WRECKS of the
RED SEA

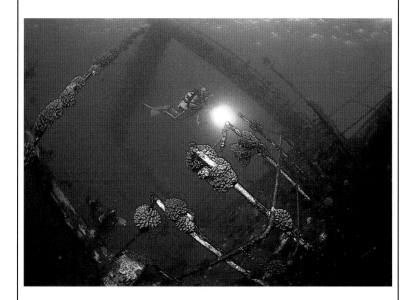

WHITE STAR
PUBLISHERS

WRECKS of the RED SEA

Texts and photographs
Andrea Ghisotti
Kurt Amsler
Roberto Rinaldi
Massimo Bicciato
Vincenzo Paolillo
Paolo Rossetti

Editorial production
Valeria Manferto
Laura Accomazzo

Illustrations and maps
Cristina Franco

Technical Consultance
Fabio Bourbon

Translation
Ann Hylands Ghiringhelli

Graphic design
Patrizia Balocco Lovisetti

Contents

INTRODUCTION by Andrea Ghisotti — page 4
1 - CEDAR PRIDE by Vincenzo Paolillo — page 18
2 - DUNRAVEN by Andrea Ghisotti — page 22
3 - THISTLEGORM by Paolo Rossetti — page 28
4 - THE CARGO BOAT AT GOBAL SHAGHIR by Roberto Rinaldi — page 46
5 - THE WRECK AT BLUFF POINT by Roberto Rinaldi — page 50
6 - GHIANNIS D. by Andrea Ghisotti — page 54
7 - CARNATIC by Andrea Ghisotti — page 62
8 - CHRISOULA K. by Kurt Amsler — page 72
9 - SEASTAR by Kurt Amsler — page 78
10 - SALEM EXPRESS by Kurt Amsler — page 84
11 - THE TUG AT ABU GALAWA by Andrea Ghisotti — page 88
12 - THE AMPHORAE AT FURY SHOAL by Andrea Ghisotti — page 92
13 - THE CARGO BOAT AT ZABARGAD by Massimo Bicciato — page 96
14 - BLUE BELL by Andrea Ghisotti — page 102
15 - PRECONTINENT II by Andrea Ghisotti — page 106
16 - UMBRIA by Andrea Ghisotti — page 112
17 - URANIA by Andrea Ghisotti — page 122
18 - NAZARIO SAURO by Andrea Ghisotti — page 130

REPRINTS:
1 2 3 4 5 6   07 06 05 04

Printed in China by Midas Printing.

The colour illustrations of the wrecks are intended as an approximate guide only: to make them clearer and avoid confusion, details such as fishing nets, ropes, lines, etc. have been left out.

1 *Although the Ghiannis D. was wrecked in relatively recent times, it is already one of the best known and most popular dive sites of the Red Sea, partly thanks to the amazingly prolific corals that envelop its structures.*
Photograph by Kurt Amsler

2 *The bow of the Umbria is now thickly encrusted with corals. The Italian cargo boat was scuttled off Port Sudan in 1940 to prevent the munitions packed in its holds from falling into enemy hands.*
Photograph by Kurt Amsler

INTRODUCTION

by Andrea Ghisotti

A - Two divers hover above the superstructures of the cargo boat at Zabargad, which lies at a depth of 25 metres. Photograph by Claudio Ziraldo

B - A diver's torch illuminates the stern of the Ghiannis D., *a Greek freighter which sank in 1983 after colliding with the reef of Sha'ab Abu Nuhâs.* Photograph by Kurt Amsler

In recent years underwater diving has enjoyed unprecedented popularity. Places once unheard-of - travelled to only by the few dauntless enthusiasts keen enough to undertake a long and adventurous journey - are now within everyone's reach. I cannot help but feel a sense of dismay and concern when I think that shipwrecks until only a few years ago undiscovered and chanced upon for the first time with incredible amazement and wonder, are within a matter of months visited by hundreds of divers, as though it were the most normal thing in the world. As in every case where a pastime or sport becomes accessible to all and sundry, precise rules are needed. Divers of the old school always looked upon a wreck as something personal, a discovery that smacked of heroism, an exploration not for the faint-hearted, which therefore entitled them to take possession of any objects they found at the site. Their approach was wrong but damage was limited since visitors were few and far between. What we need to see now is an extremely responsible, civilized attitude. Without this; wrecks are plundered and in the space of only a few months become mere empty structures of little significance. It is clear that people have to change mentality. A sunken ship is extraordinary evidence of past history, hidden for years by the sea, far more effectively than could have happened on dry land. But it is also something unique and unrepeatable, a "museum" which, were it stripped of its contents, would lose much of its significance. It is part of our heritage, a treasure which - since security guards cannot be employed beneath the ocean - is entrusted to the good sense and responsible behaviour of each individual diver. For years I have been campaigning to stop the pillaging of shipwrecks, with results that are regrettably very disappointing. But I am still optimistic: a few years ago underwater fishing appeared to be the only possible pastime, today the majority of divers would be far from shooting at the fish which, in tropical oceans, come

swimming trustingly towards them. It is also a question of intellectual curiosity: if divers know the name of a wreck, and its history, if they have perhaps done some research to find out more about it, they will no longer consider it merely an old ship with a few collectibles inside; it will instead be a piece of history to be admired and explored with respect. I want to make a special appeal to the instructors, divemasters and boatmen who accompany divers to wrecks. It is up to you to see that dives to sunken ships are only a

thrilling experience, not treasure hunts. Remember that the more a wreck remains intact, the more dives you will be able to make to it and the more customers you will have to accompany. Had the ships in the Truk Lagoon, in the Pacific Ocean, been despoiled of the incredible number of objects they contain, nobody would ever dream of making the long and very expensive journey to see the largest sunken fleet in the world. Whereas Truk earns its livelihood from tourism created by scuba diving.

C

D

C - On the sandy
seafloor at Fury
Shoal, the Roman
amphorae provide
an ideal surface for
corals to grow on.
Photograph by
Andrea Ghisotti

D - Emerging
from the gloom
is the bow of the
Carnatic, the
English steamer
wrecked on the
Sha'ab Abu Nuhās
reef in 1869.
Photograph by
Andrea Ghisotti

E - Several BSA
WDM20 motorbikes
can still be seen
inside the
Thistlegorm;
attacked during
an air raid in
October 1941,
the huge English
cargo ship went
down in the Strait
of Gobal.
Photograph by
Kurt Amsler

The Mediterranean may be considered the cradle of civilization and the first "inland sea" to be navigated in ancient times but the Red Sea follows close behind and its own maritime history is often interwoven with that of its neighbouring basin. All the oldest civilizations developed around these two seas, starting from ancient Egypt, with the Red Sea its boundary to the east and the Mediterranean to the north. Many documents tell of navigation using ancient boats made of papyrus, and the Egyptian carpenters of antiquity were renowned for their shipbuilding skills, their expertise evident in vessels like the extraordinary ship of Cheops, which has survived to the present day in its "tomb" at the foot of the pyramid of the same name. Naturally seafaring was initially limited to short voyages, mostly for coastal trade with the peoples living around the Red Sea: culturally these civilizations were far removed from the peoples of the Mediterranean and they provided a very receptive market for "Western" goods, particularly metals crafted into swords, knives and lances, and fabrics. These were traded for precious stones, ivory, pearls, elephants, spices and - sadly - slaves, the most lucrative of all trades since ancient times. Ships sailed south, as far as present-day Aden; here navigation became difficult on account of complicated winds - often headwinds - which made reaching the tempting markets of the East a problem. Navigation in the Indian Ocean was in fact regulated by the monsoonal wind system, with its seasonally reversing regime: this meant simply sailing in one direction in certain months and sailing back, again with a favourable wind, in other months. But for a long time this apparent enigma was a secret closely guarded by astute Arab and Indian merchants who, through the

E

5

centuries, controlled all ocean-going navigation bound towards India and the Far East. It is true that the Phoenicians - the most skilful and daring navigators of the ancient world - succeeded in making their own way to India, but this did not undermine the trade monopoly of the Arab merchants. Aden, called *Eudaimon* by the Romans, eventually became the thriving hub of trade in the region: densely populated, full of colour and alive with the chatter of foreign tongues, the city bustled with the comings and goings of adventurers, soldiers, sailors, traders, swindlers and harlots. Problems started when ships crammed with merchandise had to sail northwards up the Red Sea. For ten months of the year northerly winds blew gustily and the sea was constantly head on, making the going hard for vessels that were difficult to manoeuvre at the best of times, and also weighed down by their cargo. Often traders resorted to longshore navigation, transferring their goods onto more agile craft, like the *uri* used in the southern part of the Red Sea: with a simple perpendicular sail these boats managed to sail closer to the wind and take advantage of offshore breezes, seeking refuge from sudden storms among the islands scattered along the eastern side of the Red Sea. Other times, once merchandise was safely across the perilous straits of Bab el-Mandab, it travelled overland in long caravans of camels and, on reaching the Nile, continued the journey northwards by river. Many ships clearly had no option but to "tempt fate" and sail northwards: they in any case had to get to the northern ports in order to subsequently depart on new voyages. Winter - particularly the months of October and November - was the ideal time for the journey north, a fact which made trade tendentially seasonal. When these regions eventually came under Roman rule, sea trade with the East very quickly expanded. Special cargo fleets were fitted out. The port they used

as their supplies base was Berenice on the Egyptian coast, a godforsaken place with no water or decent facilities for ten months of the year, which suddenly came to life when some huge expedition was about to head south. Men had long dreamt of digging a canal to link the Mediterranean and Red seas: as early as 1300 BC Ramses II had started constructing the "Canal of the Pharaohs", which was intended to connect the eastern arm of the Nile to the Bitter Lakes; but because of insurmountable technical problems caused by windblown sand the project was abandoned. Many years later, in 106 AD, the Emperor Trajan was more

successful: *Amnis Traianus*, a navigable canal which effectively linked the Red Sea to the Mediterranean, survived for 700 years after the death of the emperor, all of seventeen centuries before the famous Suez Canal was built. With so many ships plying the waters of the Red Sea, a good many inevitably fell victim to storms, strong currents and the countless reefs. We shall never know how many thousands of ships sank there in the course of history, usually without trace! In southern Egypt are the remains of a really ancient Roman cargo vessel which probably sank after colliding with a reef, leaving tens of wine amphorae, recognizable from their characteristic elongated

A

B

A - Still lying in the holds of the Umbria, *the Italian steamship scuttled off Port Sudan in 1940, are three* Fiat 1100 Lunga *cars.*
Photograph by Franco Banfi

B - In the laundry of the Nazario Sauro, *another Italian ship that met the same fate as the* Umbria *and scuttled in the inner lagoon of Great Dahlak Island, Sudan, a two-bowl tub can still be seen.*
Photograph by Andrea Ghisotti

C

shape, scattered on the seabed. Only a short way further south is the mythical isle of Zabargad, known in antiquity as *Topazion*; here the world's most beautiful olivine was mined as early as the 15th century BC and it is possible that the vessel was heading north after putting in at the island to fill its amphorae with fine crystals of chrysolite. But there are few records of ancient shipwrecks and no serious archaeological research programmes have ever been undertaken, even though finds of antique amphorae - the most hardwearing of ancient artifacts, unspoilt by passing time - are not infrequently reported, especially along the busy coastal waters of the Sinai Peninsula. After the fall of the Western Roman Empire, local traffic resumed again. In particular, from the 7th century onwards but prevalently in the second millenium, vessels carrying pilgrims bound for Mecca travelled back and forth across the Red Sea: most of them set out from the ports of present-day Eritrea and from Suakin, the Venice of the Red Sea, home to rich merchants, smugglers and slave-traders. Years ago, on the eastern side of Sha'ab Rumi, one of Sudan's finest reefs, I discovered the remains of an unknown sunken ship at a depth of 60 metres. Its long narrow prow, typical of Arabian vessels, was decked with sea whips, their frondlike tentacles

stretching upwards, and in its hold were jars and amphorae containing what was left of a cargo that never reached its destination: one of many wrecks whose name and history are unknown. To find sunken ships with a "pedigree" we do not have to go far back in time: stories of ships wrecked in the 19th and 20th centuries, with hulls of iron, can be put together from newspaper reports of the time or from meticulous entries in the Lloyd's Register Book. During the last century maritime trade in these waters was controlled by the British, who maintained close contacts with their Indian colonies and traded throughout the East. The Suez Canal had not yet been

D

C - Adding a touch of mystery to the wreck of the Aida ll, *sunk in 1957 in the treacherous waters close to the Brothers Islands, off southern Egypt, is a puzzling, coral-encrusted object lying a short way from the vessel, at a depth of no more than 20 metres. It appears to be the remains of a late 19th century cannon, but what it is doing on the reef and where it came from no-one knows.*
Photograph by Vincenzo Paolillo

D - Leaning on its starboard flank at the foot of Hyndman Reef, near Port Safaga, is the wreck of the Salem Express, *an Egyptian ferry packed with pilgrims on their way home from Mecca. that went down in 1991.*
Photograph by Kurt Amsler

built, although many people longed for the day when it would be, excepting the British who feared their own ships would no longer have the lion's share of maritime traffic. Ships therefore sailed up the Red Sea as far as Suez where they unloaded their cargoes, which then continued northwards on amazing, interminable caravans of camels. The regular route was therefore Suez-India, the outward journey made easier by favourable winds, the return journey more of a problem as ships battled their way under sail in choppy seas, almost always against a headwind. It was for this reason that the first mixed steam-sail ships were used on these routes to the East Indies. Sails produced higher top speeds than steam and also guaranteed a reliable backup in the event of engine problems or difficulties in obtaining coal supplies. Steam navigation at last made it possible for Suez-bound vessels to reach their destination on schedule and thus ensure regular, punctual services for mail, cargo and passengers. The Suez Canal was eventually opened in 1869, amid celebrations on a grand scale. Steam navigation was by now firmly established and the dreaded shipwrecks of the past were expected to diminish. Wishful thinking... Dangerous currents, treacherous coral reefs just below the water's surface, narrow channels and warfare continued to leave the floor of the Red Sea scattered with hundreds of wrecks. Even nowadays it is not uncommon for modern ships to be stranded on its coral reefs and slowly broken up by the force of the tides. Long after the dramas lived by their seamen, the remains of these ships are explored by scuba divers for whom the experience is thrilling and interesting. Covered by the intricate lacework created by sea organisms over the years - their decks, holds, engine room and structures now a haven for countless marine creatures - the wrecks have become an integral part of the magic, silent underwater world.

A

B

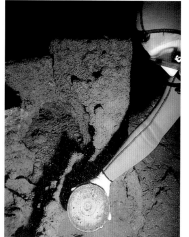

C

There is no more fascinating occupation than searching through books and archives to find out about the history of a sunken ship, either before or after actually exploring the wreck, and without such a phase the dive itself is incomplete. Even when the wrecks explored are known, information supplied by diving centres tends to be short on detail: nothing more than the name of the vessel, its nationality and a few snippets of information about how it went down. Investigating the complete history of a ship is an entirely different matter - when it was built, the routes it served, its alternating good fortune and misadventures and, lastly, its sinking, a drama which sometimes has overtones of mystery, a riddle that has often never been solved. Where to start? Your cue may come from a book or magazine which tells the tale of a famous wreck in a fairly precise area. In this case the wreck is known and you must trace its site. The best approach in this case is to chat to local people, fishermen and sailors, who are nearly always knowledgeable about past events in the vicinity. Fishermen are generally very familiar with the position of wrecks, either because fish is abundant near them or because their nets and lines can easily get caught and so fishing boats tend to keep at a distance. The search can be long and tiring and is rarely crowned with success: a suitable wreck must, after all, be resting at depths accessible to scuba divers and so close to the coast. It is essential to know the geographical coordinates of the area where the vessel sank: these can be obtained from the hydrographic offices which operate in every country, and they are often indicated on nautical maps. Once "in the field" various systems can be used to locate the site. The Global Positioning System (GPS) is the most technologically advanced. This instrument carries out triangulations with a series of satellites launched into orbit for this specific purpose: it can determine a position with an outstanding degree of accuracy,

A - A prominent "D" (standing for Danae shipping line) adorns the funnel of the Ghiannis D., a cargo which sank in the waters of Sha'ab Abu Nuhâs. Photograph by Andrea Ghisotti

B - A fundamental contribution to a wreck's identification is often made by objects discovered by divers, like the bottles, plates, bowls and jars found on the tug at Abu Galawa; only in exceptional cases, however, should anything ever be removed from the remains of sunken ships. Photograph by Andrea Ghisotti

C - The discovery of some china plates imprinted with the ship's name was a key factor in identifying the wreck of the Dunraven. Photograph by Massimo Bicciato

error varying between about twenty and a few hundred metres depending on the accuracy of the geographical coordinates and on signal reception level (signal strength is sometimes reduced for military reasons). Radar can also be used but is unlikely to be available on board small craft. Two age-old systems which are still efficient are compass readings of conspicuous points and lines of sight or alignments. The first consists of taking compass readings of a series of easily recognizable points, such as a lighthouse, a headland or the peak of a mountain which form precise angles (and so give readings in degrees) with the wreck marked on the nautical map. The second system instead consists of determining the straight lines which start from the wreck and align two conspicuous points, such as a house and a tree, a tower and a hill, and so on. Once the area where the wreck presumably lies has been located with one of these systems, the search at sea must be started, sounding the seabed with a sonic depth finder (the very high cost of more specialized equipment, like sonars and magnetometers, puts them beyond the pocket of self-financing amateurs). The search with the sonic depth finder is made by going slowly backwards and forwards until the entire search area has been covered. A more empirical method but one often used by divers in shallow water is the so-called "duck" system: this consists of being towed through the water attached to a long rope which is in turn tied to a plank serving as a diving rudder. This method can be used for a fairly thorough search to depths of about thirty metres. Once you have located a sunken ship you know nothing about or want to know more about, you must undertake the "desk research" part of your investigations. In the first case (you know nothing about the wreck) the difficulties are often insuperable, unless some useful clues have been found during its exploration. The search is usually concentrated in the holds or on the lower decks, in the hope of finding

some item belonging to the ship, with an inscription on it. Chinaware used on board ships often bears the name of the vessel or of the shipping line; the type of cargo that the ship was carrying might instead provide precious evidence. These pieces of information must be fitted together with others about the vessel, for instance, its shape, propulsion system, approximate size and the reason why it sank. With some knowledge of history, a ship's nationality can sometimes be identified by studying its cargo and its equipment and supplies. With these items of information you can start your desk research, which involves searching through Lloyd's Register Books, visiting maritime museums, writing to hydrographic offices, contacting shipping lines and ministries of the navy and merchant marine. With a lot of patience and determination, plus a generous helping of luck, you may eventually succeed in discovering the name of the ship. In the second case (the name of the sunken ship is already known), everything is simpler because the information you need to gather concerns one specific vessel. If it sank in recent times, it is possible to consult back issues of newspapers and trace survivors who might be able to give their own more detailed and accurate account of the events. The task is clearly not an easy one and plenty of enthusiasm and obstinate determination are needed to produce concrete results.

D

E

D, E - These pictures show two phases in the recovery of a pulley and the bronze bell from the Chrisoula K.: without operations of the kind it would sometimes be impossible to put a definite name to a wreck. Photograph by Kurt Amsler

F - A diver illuminates two of the distinctively shaped bottles of "London soda water" that were part of the cargo of the Carnatic. Photograph by Kurt Amsler

F

DIVING TO WRECKS

A

Diving to a wreck is one of the biggest thrills a scuba diver can experience. There are various reasons for this huge emotional impact, many of them bordering on the subconscious. The ship may have sunk in wartime or in peace, due to stormy seas, a fire, collision with a reef, sudden displacement of its cargo or ramming by another vessel - whatever the case, its wreck is the scene of a tragedy. The sea has an extraordinary ability to hide its treasures from view and to protect them against the passage of time, for much longer and more effectively than happens above the surface.

At first sight a wreck has a ghost-like appearance; after vanishing on the day it sank, it now sleeps on the seabed like a fairy-tale princess, clad in spider's webs and ornamentation created at the touch of a magic wand which made time stand still. But a closer look reveals the whole story and drama of the sinking: the gaping hole through which water poured in, displaced cargo, structures which gave way, the merchandise it was carrying, personal belongings of the crew, the propeller which stopped turning, the rudder blocked in the last direction set by the skipper, the anchors in their housings or grasping the seabed, the dramatically empty lifeboat davits, the loading tackle still hanging loose. The emotions felt by a diver are made even more intense by the huge dimensions of the vessel which - especially if the water is murky - convey a sense of intimidation and almost always make it impossible to get a complete view of the whole wreck. In addition sunken ships are sometimes located far from the coast and at a considerable depth, which means special diving techniques are needed.

These dives therefore have little in common with traditional dives to reefs: they are to be considered a specialty area of scuba diving,

requiring ad hoc training courses at which to gain familiarity with all the techniques which old divers had to learn the "do-it-yourself" way. Let's examine the problems related to this type of diving, highlighting possible dangers and all the necessary precautions. We start by looking at the equipment. Since these dives are more demanding than usual, all apparatus must be thoroughly overhauled, well tested and in efficient working order.

The demand valve must be in perfect condition, and recently serviced, and pressure tubes which show signs of weakness or wear must be replaced.

It is essential to have a spare second stage or - for instance in the tropics, where single-

B

A - In spite of the many years it has spent underwater, there are still few concretions on the huge winch that is a prominent feature on the stern of the Ghiannis D. Photograph by Alberto Muro

B - Lying at a depth of 25 metres is the huge screw of the Chrisoula K., with unusual grooves running the length of its blades. Photograph by Alberto Muro

C - The structures of the Salem Express are still relatively free of concretions, heightening the sense of tragedy conveyed by this wreck, which sank in the night between 15 and 16 December 1991, causing the death of 510 people, mostly pilgrims on their way home from Mecca. Photograph by Kurt Amsler

C

attachment valves are used - an octopus rig. Also check straps on mask and fins, lead belt buckle and buoyancy compressor (BC) feed-exhaust valves. If planning to explore the inside of the wreck, a good torch is a must and it should be an extremely dependable model. If you hope to venture into the depths of the hold, take a spare torch too, just in case the first one accidentally goes out or springs a leak. A pair of gloves serves to protect hands from rusty metal. A knife is another essential piece of equipment, to cut quickly through any nets, lines or halyards you might find yourself caught up in. When entering the deepest parts of certain "difficult" wrecks, it is important to have a reel of thread

D
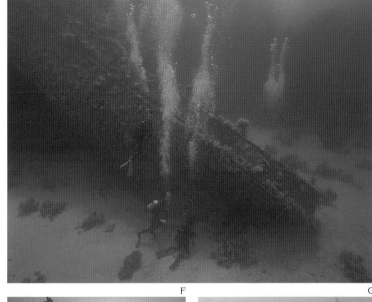

E

F

G

(several tens of metres long) to leave behind you and mark the way out. Dives to wrecks must always be planned ahead.
In the Red Sea, divers are always accompanied by divemasters from diving centres or charter boats: ask them to give you a detailed briefing before the dive, if possible providing a drawing of the vessel and information about depths and points of special interest. It is important to enter the water with fairly clear ideas about the layout of the ship, its position and the point where you will enter the water and re-surface. It is also

well worth knowing the precise history of the wreck: this makes the dive more interesting and exploration can be geared to checking out particular items of information, like the point where the ship hit the reef, the type of hole through which it took on water, the type of cargo it was carrying, etc. A quick calculation of air consumption must be made, considering the average depth of the dive, not forgetting that if the cover boat is anchored at a fixed point, your exploration will involve outward and return journeys.
In this case the available air must

D - The presence of a sunken tug by the reef at Abu Galawa is a mystery in these calm waters.
Photograph by Andrea Ghisotti

E, F - These two pictures show how, once corals have colonized the metal structures of wrecks, in a short space of time they transform them into "flowering" reefs.
Photographs by Kurt Amsler

G - Still visible on the stern of the Chrisoula K. is a light metal framework over which an awning was spread, to give some protection from the terrible heat of the sun; this is still fairly common practice on ships that ply the waters of the Red Sea.
Photograph by Vincenzo Paolillo

A

be divided by three: a third for outward journey, a third for the return journey and a third for the ascent and emergencies.

Most of the wrecks explored in the Red Sea lie against reefs or in places where the seabed is not too deep. The dive down therefore involves none of the problems encountered when wrecks are far from the coast and sites deep down on the ocean floor. When exploring a sunken vessel it is best not to slip straight into the first hold or opening spotted but to first survey the scene from a certain height so as to get a general impression of the wreck. It is then much easier to find your way around it and you will understand much more about why and how the ship sank and the present position of the vessel and its cargo. Besides, as the diver gazes in awe at the sleeping giant, it is the sight of the wreck in its entirety that conveys the strongest feelings. Only after this overview should you move closer to the structures and explore them in detail, peering through any openings you find. If the wreck is a very large one, extra care must be taken at this stage of the dive, and competent use made of your stabilizer jacket. Do not use fins when close to the seafloor: they may make the water murky, and this could cause serious problems finding the way out. Do not forget that all wrecks - including those in tropical seas - are covered internally with a thick layer of mud: the slightest movement is sufficient to stir up this mud, drastically reducing visibility. Your BC must therefore be carefully adjusted so you float midwater and, to propel yourself forward, you will often make use of your hands rather than your fins. Whenever you are about to go into a room or an opening, make sure you have already spotted a way out, which might be a window on the opposite side, a door or a hatch through which light filters. Should the room be in total darkness, you will have to leave the same way you came in. In this case it is absolutely essential not to make the water cloudy; it is sometimes a good idea to tie the end of your reel of thread

B

C

to a solid structure close to your point of entry and then gradually unwind it as you explore. Alternatively you should remain in close contact with the divemaster, who must obviously be familiar with every nook and cranny of the wreck. In this case, however, groups must be very small, not more than two or three divers with a divemaster. Should you go inside the wreck, all your equipment must be fixed to your jacket, so no depth gauges, spare valves or torches are left dangling (with the risk that they get hooked onto something).

Another problem can be caused by discharged air bubbles which "stick" to the ceiling above, making clouds of sediment rain down on the diver, possibly reducing visibility. And do not be misled by the apparent sturdiness of the vessels you explore. The structures of old wrecks are often extensively attacked and weakened by corrosion: they can sometimes give way very suddenly, especially if strong pressure created by a large quantity of air causes further strain. To be trapped or crushed by a load which has suddenly moved is not a pleasant experience!

Be particularly wary when exploring any vessel which sank in wartime. Many still contain explosives, detonators, aerial bombs, shells, missiles and the like which - in spite of the long time spent underwater - often remain potential killers. No part of the cargo must therefore be touched, let alone picked up and taken to the surface.

Keep a constant check on air consumption, and on your computer too: remember it is almost always necessary to cover the same route you took to get to the wreck, in order to reach the re-surfacing point where your boat is generally moored.

It is important to make allowance for this part of your ascent since it could be extremely dangerous to re-surface at a distance from the cover boat: there are often currents which could make it difficult or even impossible to get back to the boat.

D

E

Since the dive almost always takes you to a certain depth and it is not possible for nitrogen to be dispelled gradually during the ascent, it is essential to remain at 4-5 metres for a few minutes before re-surfacing.

This applies even when - as is to be hoped - the dive takes place within the safety limits.

After the dive, while the whole experience is still fresh in your mind, sketch a plan of the wreck in your dive book, noting down all the most important details.

This is a good way of keeping a lasting reminder of your adventure and you can also try to add more details to your drawing and notes after further dives.

D - For a diver nothing could be more thrilling than exploring the interior of the Thistlegorm; one of the trucks stowed on board can be recognized in this photograph. Photograph by Roberto Rinaldi

E - A diver rummages through the packing cases in the holds of the Umbria; the captain gave the order to scuttle the ship to prevent the vessel and its cargo of immense strategical value from falling into British hands. Photograph by Andrea Ghisotti

PHOTOGRAPHY AND VIDEO FILMING

What better souvenir of magic moments spent on a wreck than some beautiful photographs? But taking photos underwater is unfortunately far from easy: it calls for good equipment and knowledge of the techniques involved.

The big problem with wrecks is their colossal size: in photos which convey an adequate impression of the shape of the vessel and its structures, visibility often leaves much to be desired. It is common knowledge that good-quality underwater pictures have to be taken at very close range, generally between a few centimetres and 2 metres. Beyond this distance contrast and sharpness of images is notably reduced, in much the same way as when taking photographs on a foggy day on land. To try to reduce the camera-to-subject distance when taking pictures of wrecks, a very wideangle lens must be used: in the case of a *Nikonos* camera this could be the 15 or 20 mm lens (either *Nikonos* own or similar ones made by other camera manufacturers).

A recent addition to the range is the *Sea & Sea* 12 mm f-3.5 lens with a field angle of no less than 167°, which could well be the ideal choice with this camera. In the area of reflex cameras with underwater housings there is much more choice since assorted lenses can be fitted behind a special dome port designed to correct optics: 20 mm (94° like the *Nikonos* 15 mm), 18 mm (100°), 15 mm (110°) or 16 mm fish-eye (180°).

Lucky *Nikonos RS* owners can now use the new 13 mm f-2.8 fish-eye lens with a field angle of 170°. Rather than invest large sums in wideangle lenses, additional lenses can be put on the *Nikonos* standard 35 mm: this gives a satisfactory wideangle for shooting wrecks at an accessible price.

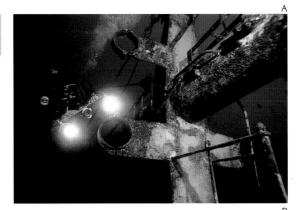

A

B

Naturally, the wider the lens angle, the closer you can go to your subject, with better results in terms of image sharpness. Fish-eye lenses can nonetheless create a distortion problem, because they cause very obvious deformation around the edges of the frame, making straight lines curved. A shot taken of the wreck may therefore look deformed and, in the case of close-ups, not at all realistic; for this reason it is often better to use lenses with not such a wide angle, which keep lines perpendicular even at the edges of the frame.

Because shots are always taken at a certain distance from the wreck, flash is a hindrance rather than a help. The light would not illuminate the structures but would instead light up particles suspended in the water between photographer and subject, causing a serious loss of quality. Ambient light is therefore best. If the wreck lies in shallow water where light is still strong, there are no big problems.

Move to a midwater position adjusting your BC so you are

neutrally buoyant and still; focus, making sure you are not facing directly into the light (overexposure would blank out part of the vessel), set the right exposure and, holding the camera firmly in both hands, press the shutter release.

It is always worth taking several shots with different apertures, especially if you are using the automatic exposure control since this rarely reproduces the true blue or green colour of the sea, generally tending towards overexposure. When deciding on your shot, do not focus downwards as this makes the structures look flat against the background and gives insufficient contrast. It is better to take the picture from the side of the subject or looking slightly upwards. When it comes to choosing film, use the least sensitive: these give better results in terms of etching, absence of grain and image contrast.

Things get more difficult when the wreck is located at much greater depth, and more and more light is filtered out by the water. Even with maximum diaphragm aperture, the light will often be insufficient and shutter speed must be adjusted. The slowest time with the *Nikonos* is 1-30th second; using the automatic meter control, it can be made even slower but one cannot know exactly how much. With underwater reflex cameras or with the *Nikonos RS* there are instead no limitations and even slower times can be used. Movement remains a risk and the camera must be held very still; the subject of the shot must also be motionless.

A possible alternative is to use more sensitive film but the image obtained is not as sharp.

Not only general views should be shot on a wreck.

There is a whole range of possible medium-distance shots and close-ups, to produce pictures of details of the ship, its fixtures and fittings and its cargo. Here too a wideangle lens is used but this time with flash - or better still, two flash units - to adequately cover the very wide field angle. Taking shots of the external structures of the vessel presents no special problems and normal photographic techniques can be used (though remember to use smaller angle lenses to get good pictures of the many fish, invertebrates and crustaceans that come into view).

Taking photographs inside the wreck is a completely different matter: visibility is much reduced or even nil, making conditions similar to those encountered when taking photos at night. Flash lighting is needed to illuminate the scene, together with torchlight to adjust camera settings. Luckily the metal structures of the vessel give off a certain amount of reflected light and illumination is less of a problem than at nighttime on land.

But pay special attention to suspended particles: make only the gentlest of movements and drift midwater with your stab jacket correctly adjusted, otherwise you can wave your photos goodbye!

C - Because of the immense size of wrecks, if pictures are taken from a distance there is always the risk of reducing contrast and sharpness of images; to try to keep camera-to-subject distance as short as possible, a very wideangle lens must therefore be used. The image shows a diver taking pictures of a deck section of the Zabargad cargo ship.
Photograph by Massimo Bicciato

D - Taking pictures of the fish usually encountered amid the metal plates of wrecks presents no particular problems: good light is all that is needed. Here the camera of a diver has captured a shoal of glassfish swimming among the Carnatic structures.
Photograph by Kurt Amsler

Video filming a wreck involves far fewer problems. Video cameras work well even where light conditions are poor, and so can be successfully used in very deep water. The continuity of the images means that the wreck can be visually "described" by shooting it from closer distances than is possible with photographs, thus avoiding difficult panoramic views.

Here too wideangle lenses are needed: the solution usually adopted is to fit an additional wideangle on the standard zoom which, even with focal length at a minimum, cannot give satisfactory angles of field. Many of the housings now produced have, as a standard fitting, an additional wideangle lens behind a special correcting port; this system makes it possible to take marvellous panoramic shots with excellent depth of field. In this case too illumination is still a problem. Spotlights are heavy, expensive, have a limited running time, and only give light and colour to foreground objects. The best solution is to get your subject to hold a 100-250 watt spot, thereby halving the distance the light has to travel (subject-videocamera instead of videocamera-subject-videocamera). Make sure he knows he must never point the spot straight at the camera: the resulting overexposure would be disastrous.

Rather than shoot endless scenes that have little real point to them, it is best to plan the sequences you want to film - discussing them with your subject and doing a few trial runs - before your descent into the water.

If you are instead alone or with divers you have not previously met, there is no option but to mount lights on the camera housing: in this case watch out for suspended particles, using articulated arms to position the light away from the camera, at a right angle to it, and never shoot with artificial light in places where another diver has passed by and made the water extremely cloudy.

LIFE ON THE WRECKS

The housing shortage may reach desperate levels in the huge, overcrowded cities of our planet but competition for space is far worse underwater; any new object which descends to the seafloor is instantly invaded by "squatters" of the marine habitat, a multitude of organisms aspiring to make it their home. The often huge dimensions of a wreck and its endless structures, rooms, niches, nooks and crannies make it a paradise for marine flora and fauna. They quickly take possession and before long turn plates of metal and super structures into a fantastic garden embellished with ornamentation in breathtaking colours. Among the most contented new residents are the cnidarians: since their food is carried by the current, they settle on the most exposed structures. The highly colourful alcyonarians are among the fastest to grow and colonize the wreck, occupying spots where they are strategically well placed to ensnare whatever prey the current brings them. Gorgonians and hard corals take longer to grow, but only relatively longer: on the "hangar" of Jacques Cousteau's *Soucoupe Plongeante*, in the *Precontinent II* village at Sha'ab Rumi, a coral "roof" has grown to a size of over a square metre in as little as 20 years. Older wrecks in tropical seas are completely covered by a hard coral "crust" which, with the passing years, incorporates their metal structures, with a camouflage that transforms them beyond all recognition. Besides the sessile organisms which coat its surfaces, every wreck becomes densely populated with an enormous variety of marine fauna - fish, crustaceans, sea urchins, mollusks - all totally at home in what might initially have seemed an alien environment.

In parts where there is more light parrotfish are often found: they nibble at encrusted coral, making a characteristic noise which can be clearly heard if you hold your breath. Wrecks in fairly shallow water teem with all the minor fauna typical of barrier reefs: schools of damselfish, surgeonfish, anthias, wrasses and pairs of butterflyfish, as well as occasional eye-catching angelfish and triggerfish. The most inaccessible corners are the favourite haunts of morays which sometimes grow to a colossal size; they share their dens with small teams of cleaner shrimps which tend to their "grooming" and devour the proceeds. Holds, air-ducts and darker places are inhabited by large scorpionfish which have highly toxic poison in their vicious fin spines and should therefore be

approached with caution. Their companions in the murky depths - members of the same Scorpaenidae family - are often impressive turkeyfish, harmless provided contact with their venomous fin spikes is avoided. A diver exploring the engine room and the darkest parts of the holds instead has every chance of finding himself face to face with a "wall" formed of a colony of glass-fish, nocturnal fish which habitually gather in huge schools.

Lying right at the bottom of the holds, so well camouflaged as to pass unnoticed, crocodilefish - so-called on account of their flattened shape and large mouth - often make their homes. These fish are totally innocuous to man and divers occasionally find a pair of them in an affectionate "embrace",

the head of one resting on the body of the other. If the still silence of a wreck is not too often disturbed by visiting divers, there is every possibility of spotting twinspot snappers: these large, powerful predators, high up in the underwater food chain, swim midwater where groups of barracuda and jacks also gather. But in and around wrecks the unchallenged "king of the castle" is the grouper. You are bound to catch sight of these fairly heavy-bodied fish swimming back and forth amid holds and superstructures, with a menacing air befitting their fame as predators. Occasionally on isolated wrecks a truly enormous grouper - weighing even as much as 100 kilos - comes into view. Known for their longevity, they have a strong sense of territory and are therefore to be considered rightful guardians of the sunken ships they adopt. Diving to a wreck at night is a fascinating experience since it offers a chance to see nocturnal fauna mostly hidden from view by day. One such creature is the diadema sea urchin with long black or grey spines which wave threateningly as any intruder approaches.

Special care needs to be taken with *Asthenosoma varium*, a deceptively attractive little red sea urchin, with tiny white globules on its short spines: as any imprudent diver who picks one up will discover to his cost, these globules contain a strong venom which can cause severe pain.

Graceful sea lilies adorn the wrecks, as do serpent stars with many-branched arms which coil up if the light of a torch is shone on them. Not easy to spot by day, at night they come into their own, along with whole processions of prawns, crabs, brightly coloured sea slugs and marine snails, like the lovely cowrie. All invertebrates which feed on plankton have their polyps dilated at night; other creatures like the crinoids move about on the sea fans and coral reefs. Together they create a riot of colours and forms that makes even the most insignificant sunken vessel look like a fun fair.

D

E

F

G

A - Alcyonarians are definitely the most abundant and spectacular of the soft corals that grow in profusion on the wrecks of the Red Sea. The picture shows the vivid colours of soft corals growing on the Ghiannis D.. Photograph by Alberto Muro

B - This photograph highlights the infinite variety of marine life of the Bluff Point wreck. Photograph by Alberto Muro

C - The wreck of the Jolanda *has now been transformed into an artificial reef populated by large schools of anthias.* Photograph by Roberto Rinaldi

D - A coral grouper swims in the midst of a dense school of anthias on the Aida *wreck.* Photograph by Franco Banfi

E - Sweetlips are regular visitors to the Jolanda wreck. Photograph by Roberto Rinaldi

F - Soft corals of spectacular dimensions present divers to the Aida *with a stunning sight.* Photograph by Franco Banfi

G - Face to face with a turkeyfish on the wreck of the Dunraven; *this splendid marine creature should be approached with caution since its rays are poisonous.* Photograph by Roberto Rinaldi

CEDAR PRIDE
by Vincenzo Paolillo

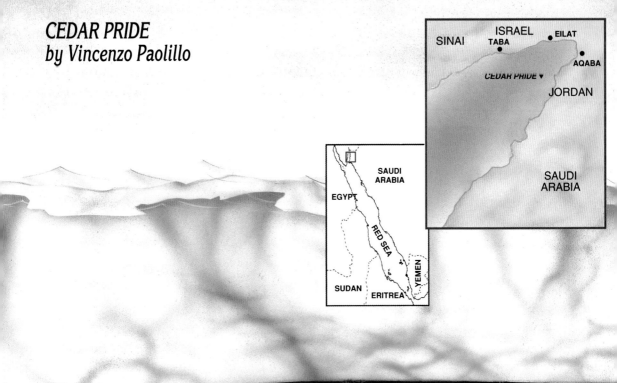

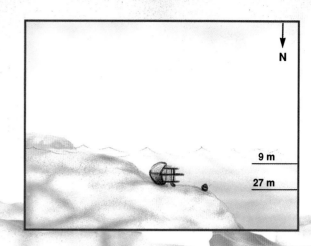

RATINGS

Finding site: easy.
Visibility: excellent.
Current: none.
Dive difficulty: easy.
Presence of lines or nets: none.
Historical interest: low.
Photographic interest: medium.
Biological interest: high.

DATA FILE

Type of wreck: cargo ship.
Nationality: Lebanese.
Year of construction: 1964.
Tonnage: 1,161 tons.
Date of sinking: spring of 1986.
Cause of sinking: sunk for tourist
        purposes.
Site position: south of the port
        of Aqaba.
Distance from shore: less than
        100 metres.
Minimum depth: 9 metres.
Maximum depth: 27 metres.

THE CARGO BOAT
CEDAR PRIDE

One of the most colourful wrecks of the whole Red Sea, the *Cedar Pride*, is situated just a short way from the shores of Aqaba, almost opposite Jordan's only port. This huge freighter was originally called the *San Bruno* and was registered with Lloyd's as sailing under the Greek flag. Early in 1982 it was purchased by a Lebanese shipping line to carry raw materials, and was given a new name. Its new activity was shortlived: in July of the same year, while loading fertilizers (phosphates and potassium) for export to Iraq, the boat was suddenly rocked by an explosion in the engine room. A terrible fire broke out, made all the worse by the highly inflammable cargo, and it took days for the teams of firefighters who rushed to the scene to extinguish the flames. Although completely burnt-out, the *Cedar Pride* did not sink, however: its ugly carcass, totally useless and abandoned by both its owners and insurers, was left moored in the harbour, occupying precious space. Nobody knew quite what to do with it. Then one day Jordan's WWF association contacted King Hussein - who often spends holidays in Aqaba - and proposed towing the *Cedar Pride* out to sea and sinking her, with the objective of turning the remains of the ship into an artificial reef. The king was enthusiastic and gave the scheme his approval. In the spring of 1986, after any fuel still on board had been removed so as not to pollute the seabed, the carcass was towed a few kilometres south of the port and sunk with explosives. The wreck now lies less than 100 metres from the shore, between 9 and 27 metres deep. No more brilliant solution could have been found: perhaps due to unusual currents or to the unexpected chemical reaction of the few phosphates left on board, in a short space of time the metal structures were transformed by an explosion of

A,C - Not far from the stern of the Cedar Pride lies a smaller, nameless wreck; its elegant line makes it seem likely the craft was used to carry tourists. After exploring the Cedar Pride, it is worth sparing time to pay a visit also to this boat.

B - The name Cedar Pride is still clearly legible on the freighter's stern, but before being purchased by a Lebanese shipping line, it sailed under the Greek flag and was registered with Lloyd's as the San Bruno.

D - The metal structures of the Lebanese cargo boat were very quickly colonized by a myriad of multi-coloured corals, their growth possibly encouraged by nutrient-rich currents or a chemical reaction between the salt water and the few phosphates left on board.

colours, remarkable growths of coral branches, sponges and - making the biggest visual impact of all - alcyonarians of an incredible size.

Diving to the wreck

The relatively shallow water, with no strong currents, makes this a problem-free dive but nonetheless an interesting one: the midsection in particular, at a depth of about 20 metres, can easily be explored by less experienced divers. The visit to the *Cedar Pride* can be started from the beach; alternatively your boat can be anchored to one of the pieces of the freighter that just reach the surface. If you are approaching the wreck from the beach, follow the sandy bottom, dotted with sea urchins. For over half the distance the water is no more than 2 metres deep, then the seafloor slopes more steeply - for about 80 metres - as far as the wreck. You will see the vessel resting on its port flank with bows pointing upwards and mast facing west: right in the middle of the hull the reef has an opening - a kind of pass - which makes it easy to explore the ship thoroughly. Its superstructures point out to sea and one of the lifeboats, now corroded by the salt water, is lying on the seabed. Against a breathtaking backdrop of large sea anemones, corals, sponges and splendid alcyonarians, the ubiquitous scalefin anthias swim to and fro, together with some impressive examples of Napoleon fish and - if you are lucky - the occasional turtle. It is worth spending part of your dive exploring another wreck, lying about 50 metres from the stern of the *Cedar Pride*, towards the open sea in a south-east direction: it is a small, elegantly shaped vessel, possibly a tourist boat. If you are lucky it is possible to see a crocodilefish that had taken up residence inside the small boat.

E

F

G

E - Several brightly coloured soft corals adorn the massive three-blade screw propeller of the Cedar Pride.

F - The slender form of the stempost is now partly hidden from view by profusely growing branches of multi-coloured alcyonarians.

G - A prominent feature of a bathroom in the crew's quarters is this bathtub: an incongruous scene made to look even odder by the great numbers of anthias swimming to and fro around it.

All the photographs of the dive to the Cedar Pride *were taken by Vincenzo Paolillo.*

21

DUNRAVEN
by Andrea Ghisotti

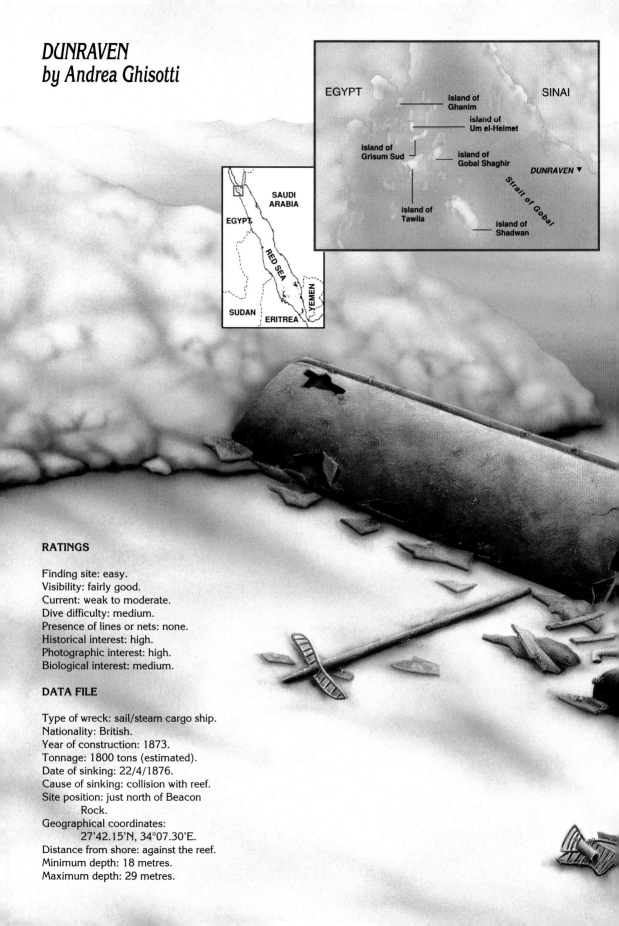

EGYPT   SINAI

island of Ghanim

island of Um el-Heimet

island of Grisum Sud

island of Gobal Shaghir

DUNRAVEN ▼

island of Tawila

island of Shadwan

Strait of Gobal

SAUDI ARABIA

EGYPT

RED SEA

SUDAN   ERITREA   YEMEN

RATINGS

Finding site: easy.
Visibility: fairly good.
Current: weak to moderate.
Dive difficulty: medium.
Presence of lines or nets: none.
Historical interest: high.
Photographic interest: high.
Biological interest: medium.

DATA FILE

Type of wreck: sail/steam cargo ship.
Nationality: British.
Year of construction: 1873.
Tonnage: 1800 tons (estimated).
Date of sinking: 22/4/1876.
Cause of sinking: collision with reef.
Site position: just north of Beacon
       Rock.
Geographical coordinates:
       27'42.15'N, 34°07.30'E.
Distance from shore: against the reef.
Minimum depth: 18 metres.
Maximum depth: 29 metres.

THE CARGO BOAT *DUNRAVEN*

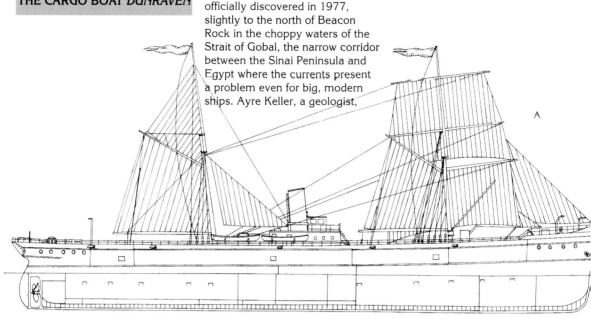

The wreck of the *Dunraven* was officially discovered in 1977, slightly to the north of Beacon Rock in the choppy waters of the Strait of Gobal, the narrow corridor between the Sinai Peninsula and Egypt where the currents present a problem even for big, modern ships. Ayre Keller, a geologist,

A

B

A - This drawing shows the Dunraven as she must have looked shortly after completion in 1873, in a Newcastle-on-Tyne shipyard.

B - In 1978 a lucky find - a plate like this one - made it possible to identify the wreck: inscribed in clear letters on the white porcelain is the name Dunraven. Photograph by Massimo Bicciato

came across the sunken ship while doing surveying work for an oil company and immediately informed Howard Rosenstein who, for the previous ten years or so, had run an important diving centre in the area. But Keller's indications were very vague and it was not until much later and almost by chance, when accompanying a group of German scuba divers on a dive, that Rosenstein actually found the wreck. There was no trace of a name and for almost a year the wreck was explored without concrete results; lots of broken crockery was found, together with objects retrieved from the holds, but nothing that could help reconstruct the history of the vessel. There was all sorts of speculation about the identity of the ship. Its shape was very like that of the ships used by Lawrence of Arabia - the *Dufferin*, *Suva*, *Harding* and *M-31* - to take precious treasures from Suez to Aqaba, to finance the Arab rebellion against the Turks. Had this been the case, its holds should have contained a real treasure trove, but the divers who searched at length came away empty-handed. Another trail led to a mysterious "Q" class British warship, sent to the Middle East on a top secret mission during the

first World War. It was only in November 1978 that, at long last, the name *Dunraven* came to light, inscribed in pale blue at the centre of a fine-quality porcelain plate, and before long other plates with the same inscription were found. Now that the name of the ship was known, Lloyd's would be able to fill in on its history.

But instead of getting simpler, the mystery thickened. Two *Dunravens* were listed in the Lloyd's Register books. The first, built in 1890, had subsequently changed name to *Sara Radcliff*, and had been torpedoed and sunk in the Atlantic in 1917. The second had been converted to a British "Q" class ship - i.e. a "pirate" ship which sailed as a cargo boat but was fitted out as a warship - and used to hunt German submarines, under the new name of *Marshal*. At the outset of the first World War, it was seriously damaged in battle; for their bravery in combat its Captain Gordon Campbell and part of the crew received the Victoria Cross. The ship was later sunk in the Channel. So neither of the two *Dunravens* could be the one lying in the Strait of Gobal unless the Lloyd's entries had been falsified to cover the secret mission of the mysterious pirate ship. And a request from the British Admiralty gave further support to this theory: it was asked that all dives to the wreck be suspended, since the sunken vessel could be a British "war cemetery". Meanwhile news of the wreck was spreading and the BBC sent a film crew to shoot a documentary for "The World around us" series: their cameramen spent several weeks exploring and filming the site. Suggestions as to the real identity of ship became more and more fanciful. According to some, it was a Dutch ship, named after the Nordic town of the same name. Other people thought about the elegant chinaware found in the wreck and wondered whether

C

D

E

to the region for the first time in 1910, about half a century after the probable sinking of the ship. Also written on the china plates inscribed with the name *Dunraven* were the initials GFB: these were found to belong to George F. Barnes, winner of the first prize for chinaware design at a London exhibition in 1873. This fact, together with the closing of Webb's factory in 1880, meant that the period of time in which the ship had sunk was reduced to seven years. The mystery was now close to being solved and the final piece of evidence came from the Maritime Museum in Newcastle, where news of the ship was finally found. The *Dunraven* was a mixed

it could be the private yacht of the American millionaire Randolph Hearst, owner of Dunraven Castle in Wales. A sudden turning-point in the investigations came when a find was made in the hold: bottles of an unusual double-curved shape, made of thick, greenish glass, bearing the inscription: "Webb's Double Soda and Other Waters. By appointment to Her Majesty the Queen. Islington, London". It did not take long to find out that the firm which produced the bottles of soda water had started business in 1836 and closed in 1880. The queen in question had to be Victoria, who had come to the throne in 1837. All dreams of riches vanished, since Lawrence of Arabia came

F

C - As is evident from this photo, the sinking ship overturned and came to rest on the sea floor with the keel pointing upwards.
Photograph by Andrea Ghisotti

D - Lying at a depth of 28 metres, the stern is undoubtedly the best conserved and most interesting part of the wreck.
Photograph by Andrea Ghisotti

E - The large screw with its long, narrow blades looks considerably different from the much more compact screws fitted on ships today; like many vessels built in the late 19th century, the Dunraven had traditional sails as well as a steam-propelled engine.
Photograph by Kurt Amsler

F - The wreck is home to countless fish of numerous species: prominent on account of their markings are sergeant scissortails which gather in dense shoals.
Photograph by Massimo Bicciato

steam-sail vessel - 82 metres long, 9.7 metres wide - launched in 1873 by C. Mitchell & C. Iron Ship Builders in Newcastle on Tyne, for use on the route to India via Suez. It sank on a return voyage from Bombay to Newcastle, with a cargo of wool and cotton. During the night of April 22nd 1876 it hit the southernmost tip of the Sha'ab Mahmûd reef, where a beacon (hence the name of Beacon Rock given to this tip of the reef) now warns passing vessels of the danger lurking beneath the surface. The cargo caught fire and burned for 13 hours until the doomed vessel turned over and sank to a depth of 25 metres. Considering how much time passed before it sank, there was probably no loss of life, although bones found in the hold were identified by a doctor from Sharm el-Sheikh as definitely those of a child. His opinion was challenged by another doctor who said they belonged to a pig. The answer was provided by examining the construction plans of the ship: the area where the bones were found was in fact a pig pen.

A - The silhouette of a diver is visible through the screw aperture, now so thickly encrusted with corals as to be hardly recognizable. Photograph by Alberto Muro

B - What remains of the huge funnel is now lying on the seabed, a convenient shelter for the many fish which are now permanent inhabitants of the wreck. Photograph by Andrea Ghisotti

C - A diver peers into the biggest hole ripped open in the midships section of the hull on the fatal night of April 22, 1876 when the Dunraven collided with the Sha'ab Mahmud reef; at the bottom of the picture one can see the half-open valves of a large clam. Photograph by Andrea Ghisotti

Diving to the wreck

Diving to the *Dunraven* involves no particular difficulties since the vessel lies at a maximum depth of about 29 metres. It is best to start exploring the wreck from the stern and gradually make your way towards the bow, which is deeper down. Your boat should be anchored at a special buoy, positioned slightly to north-east: from here the point where you will make your descent can easily be reached with a rubber dinghy. The water is not always very clear because a strong current - particularly if northerly - tends to stir up fragmental material on the seafloor. If visibility is good, as soon as you start your descent you catch sight of the outline of the huge ship, lying upside down on the seafloor with its keel facing upwards. The stern is perhaps the part most intact and - with its huge screw and its rudder decked with soft corals - most visually impressive. At the point where the stern touches the seabed the water is about 28 metres deep. You can enter the hull through three gaping holes in the starboard flank which hit the reef; the port side is instead much better conserved. The interior is quite dark but shafts of light filter through the various openings. It is nonetheless essential to have a good torch, also because the remains of the cargo are well worth a closer look. In the direction of the stern you can make out some old hemp or coir ropes, as well as a few bales of cotton that were part of the cargo; after the thoughtless plundering during the early years after the discovery, there is little left of the bottles and china. The wreck is inhabited by huge groupers - sometimes weighing as much as 50 kilos -, large scorpionfish and amusing crocodilefish. You can move towards the bow inside the wreck since there are plenty of openings through which to get out.

Don't forget to visit the midships section where the engine room used to be: here you will find a tangle of contorted metal but the huge funnel and a few air-ducts are still clearly visible in its midst. On the seafloor lie the two metal masts, their rigging now encrusted with coral; the crow's nest is in an excellent state of conservation and is worth taking a look at.

Fish swim constantly to and from around the wreck and, if you bide your time, you have every chance of thrilling encounters with barracuda, mantas and eagle rays. The bow section is instead in rather poor condition.

It is best reached from the interior, where huge schools of silver fish form almost solid, shining walls which open up to let divers swim through. Exit is possible from the bow, through a hole in the flank, but the gap is fairly narrow and so you have best make your way out slightly sooner. The bow is lying right up against the reef, in about 18 metres of water.

D - The crow's nest can still be spotted amid the remains of one of the masts, now resting on the sea floor.
Photograph by Andrea Ghisotti

E - After more than a century under water much of the interior has been reduced to debris and there are thick layers of sediment, but many structural elements - like these wooden steps - are still recognizable.
Photograph by Andrea Ghisotti

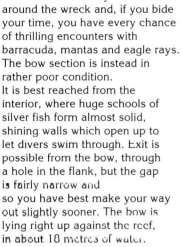

F - Although most of the cargo was destroyed by the fire that broke out on board after the collision in April 1876 or was carried off by trophy-hunters in the years following the discovery of the wreck, in the holds one still comes across ropes, bales of cotton and - as in this case - old wooden crates.
Photograph by Andrea Ghisotti

G - An enormous branch of soft coral grows on one of the ribs of the hull, at this point severely damaged.
Photograph by Massimo Bicciato

H - Inside the holds dwell several shoals of luminescent glassfish, always a captivating sight. Caught in the beam of divers' torches their bodies gleam and the gloomy scene is momentarily transformed by reflected silvery light.
Photograph by Roberto Rinaldi

THISTLEGORM
by Paolo Rossetti

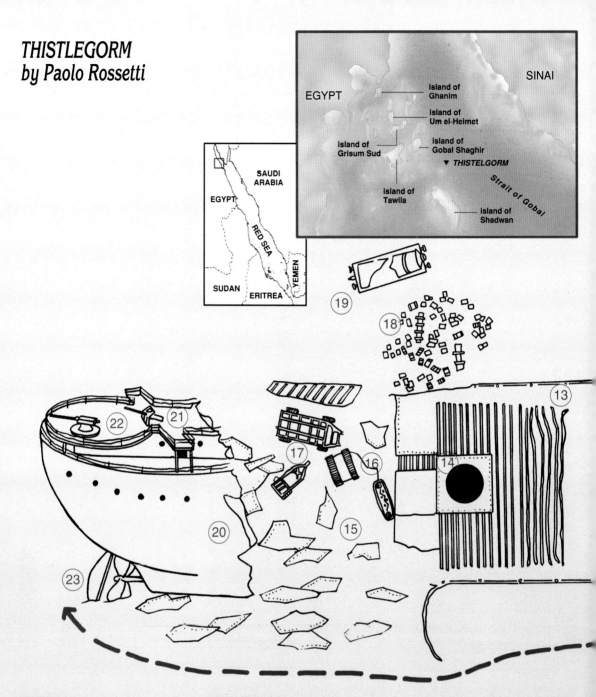

RATINGS

Finding site: medium to high difficulty.
Visibility: usually good.
Current: sometimes very strong.
Dive difficulty: medium to high.
Presence of lines or nets: none.
Historical interest: high.
Photographic interest: high.
Biological interest: medium.

DATA FILE

Type of wreck: cargo ship.
Nationality: British.
Year of construction: 1940.
Tonnage: 9,009 tons.
Date of sinking: 6/10/1940.
Cause of sinking: air raid.
Site position: in the Strait of Gobal, between Sha'ab Ali reef and the Sinai coast.
Distance from shore: about 8 miles.
Minimum depth: 18 metres.
Maximum depth: 31 metres.

1 - The foredeck looks still well preserved.

2 - The port anchor is hanging from the hawsehole whereas the chain of the starboard anchor continues northwards for 60 metres or so.

3 - The anchor windlasses are in an excellent condition, with very limited concretion on the chains.

4 - Close to the cargo hatch of No. 1 hold are two tanks truck.

5 - The No. 1 hold has two loading levels. Stacked below are boxes containing medical supplies, Lee Enfield Mk III rifles and spare parts, electricity generators, aircraft parts, camp-beds for field hospitals, rubber boots and tyres; above are several Morris cars and numerous BSA model WDM20 motorcycles.

6 - Secured in place at the level of the main mast are two paravanes. These torpedo-like devices fitted with large balance tabs served to sever cables mooring contact mines.

7 - The main mast, with the distinctly evident crosstrees which supported the lights and radio antennas, has fallen onto the deck.

8 - Visible at the base of the mast are the winches used when manoeuvring the cargo booms.

9 - The interior of hold No. 2 is also split into two levels. Underneath are a number of Bedford trucks, loaded with motorcycles; on top are lots more BSA motorbikes and some Morris cars.

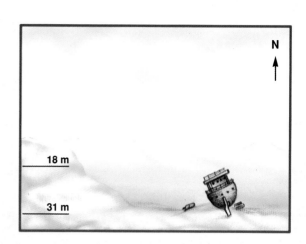

N

18 m

31 m

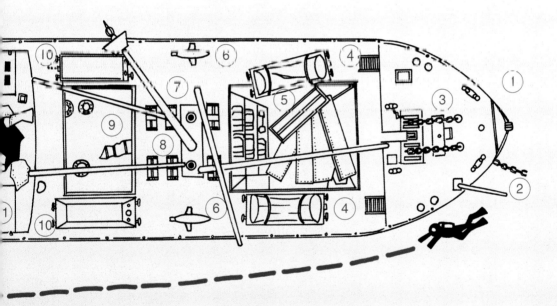

10 - There are two railway wagons close to the entrance to the second hold; their weight has caused damage to the deck structures and great caution is therefore necessary when exploring the hold.

11 - The decking on the bridge has almost entirely disappeared and it is possible to get into the captain's quarters through the gaping holes.

12 - Aircraft bombs, anti-tank mines and artillery shells are stacked on the lower level of No. 3 hold while above - in rows - are hundreds of boxes containing light munitions, land mines and hand grenades.

13 - Between the deck and funnel, the bridge had been partly protected by sheet-metal roofing, much of which has now disintegrated.

14 - The huge funnel has now collapsed: all that is left is a large hole with pieces of bent metal around it.

15 - The ship appears to have been sliced into two at the height of No. 4 hold, the point where the German bombs struck their target. Scattered all around are wreckage and remains of the cargo, mostly ammunition and assorted explosive devices.

16 - Easily distinguished among the twisted metal plating are two small armoured vehicles, Mk II Bren Carrier, made by Vicker-Armstrong: weighing only 4.5 tons, these light tanks were among the most efficient "all-rounder" vehicles used during World War II.

17 - Also in the holds of the Thistlegorm were several carts used to transport bombs.

18 - Flung all over the seabed are aerial bombs, large explosive devices, tens of cases of anti-tank mines, ammunition and hand grenades, as well as assorted mechanical parts, all jumbled together with twisted girders and pieces of wreckage.

19 - About 20 metres from the wreck, on the left-hand side, are the remains of one of the two locomotives that were being transported on deck, above hold No. 4.

20 - The stern section lies about fifteen metres form the rest of the vessel.

21 - Installed behind the cannon was a heavy fixed-position machine-gun.

22 - On the poop deck the 120 mm cannon is still fixed on its mount, at the centre of a circular stand.

23 - On the sea floor the rudder and screw are almost entirely visible above the sand.

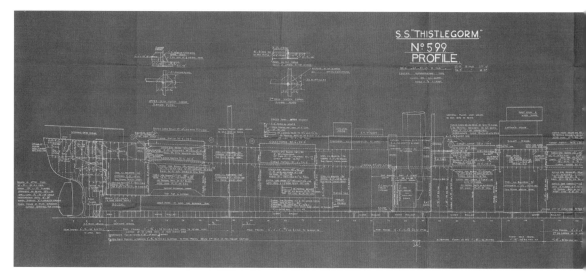

S.S. "THISTLEGORM."
N° 599
PROFILE

"It was very hot that night and for the first time since our departure I got completely undressed before climbing into my bunk. I was still half-awake when I felt a terrible explosion and heard the bosun shouting up on deck. I tried to get up. It was dark in the cabin; my things were all in a pile and I couldn't find my clothes, so I went up on deck with nothing but my lifejacket on. There was an inferno of flames and flashes all around me and the way to the lifeboats was blocked; I thought the best way to save myself was to dive into the water. I dashed over to the railing; it was already boiling hot.

I was about to jump when I turned and saw one of the gunners lying unconscious, with flames all over him. I ran towards him but the deck was covered with pieces of glass that stuck in my feet so, before I could pick him up, I had to stop and take them out. I managed to get the man up onto my shoulders and was trying get

across the burning deck to the lifeboat when I heard someone calling. I saw Jon Dagg, the second officer, coming towards us with some other men; with their help we at last managed to get into the lifeboat".

In this account published in the Stornoway Gazette in 1943 Angus Macleay, a bridge-man on the *Thistlegorm*, tells of the terrible moments that followed the explosion on board the British cargo ship during the night of October 5, 1943. The *Thistlegorm* had been launched in Sunderland, in England, on April 9, 1940. Built in the shipyards of J.L. Thompson & Sons, the vessel was 131 metres in length and had a gross tonnage of 9,009 tons. Owned by Albyn Line Ltd., it had a triple expansion, three-cylinder engine (the cylinders, each of a different volume, received pressure from coal-fired boilers and transmitted movement to the drive shaft which turned at 57 r.p.m.): it was capable of producing 1,860

A - Shown here is one of the original building plans of the Thistlegorm, *a document now of notable interest.* Photograph by Paolo Rossetti

B - Dated June 25, 1940, this document is evidence of the registration of the Thistlegorm *in the British register of shipping, entered here are, among other things, the technical characteristics of the ship, the name of the shipyard where it was built and that of its owner, Albyn Line Ltd.* Photograph by Paolo Rossetti

C - The archive photograph is of the launch of the Thistlegorm, *in Sunderland on April 9, 1940.* Photograph by Paolo Rossetti

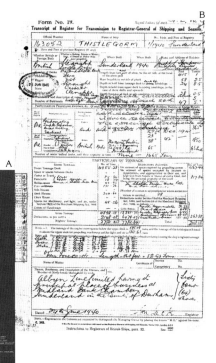

B

A

horsepower giving a speed of 10.5 knots. The *Thistlegorm* (the name means "blue thistle" in Gaelic) was registered with Lloyds in the 100 A.1 class; because of the war, it was armed with a 4.7 inch cannon, an anti-aircraft machine-gun mounted on a tower and a transportable heavy machine-gun. Its first mission was to North America, with a cargo of aircraft parts and railway rails. On the second it sailed as far as the East Indies, and on the third to Argentina: both these voyages were made to bring back a full load of foodstuffs. On its fourth mission - tragically destined to be the last - the *Thistlegorm* left Glasgow in the first week in September, destined for the Red Sea. After a brief stop in Cape Town to take on coal (the temporary closure of the Suez Canal had forced it to take the longer route), the ship headed north east; it had sailed the length of the Red Sea and reached the Strait of Gobal when, at 1.30 a.m. on the morning of October 6,

C

(left) Angus Macleay
(above) His medals (left to right), George Medal, 1939-1945 Star, Atlantic Star, Africa Star, War Medal 1939-1945 and Lloyd's War Medal
(R. J. Scarlett)

1941, it was attacked by the enemy and sank. The dramatic sequence of events - the explosion, abandoning ship and the sinking itself - is still vividly recalled by Harry Bansall, the ship's third engine-room officer: "Jack Blair, the first engineer, was at the helm of one of the two lifeboats drawing away from the huge, burning ship. But he was still staring at the *Thistlegorm*, his eyes glued to the horrific scene: in the holds boxes of light ammunition and hand grenades were exploding like fireworks. Great tongues of fire shot skywards, lighting up the still "shellshocked" faces of the men on the lifeboat: besides myself

A - Angus Macleay was a member of the crew of the Thistlegorm at the time of its tragic sinking; although himself wounded, he succeeded in rescuing a fellow seaman from the flames and carrying him to safety; shown here at the side of his portrait, taken after the war, are the decorations he received for bravery.
Photograph by Paolo Rossetti

there was Ray Gibson, the 18 year-old telegraph operator, on his second voyage, Joe Dagg, third bridge officer, and Angus Macleay, bridge-man, injured but alive. 'Skipper, let's get moving!' yelled one of the men to Blair: totally absorbed by the scene, he had practically turned the head of the lifeboat towards the dying ship. The HMS Carlisle was anchored a few hundred metres from the site of the disaster; the two lifeboats

reached its side practically simultaneously and the men were still climbing on board when the light from a tremendous explosion turned night into day and the *Thistlegorm* was clearly visible, broken in two by the blast, as she sank beneath the water. When Captain William Ellis came aboard the *Carlisle* we did a quick count to see if anyone was missing: we discovered that five

B - Although not the most widely used of the heavy German bombers deployed in World War Two, the Heinkel He 111 was definitely the most famous; the Thistlegorm sank after being attacked by a squadron of planes similar to the one shown here.
Photograph by Paolo Rossetti

C - The young man in this snapshot is Harry Bansall, third engine-room officer on board the Thistlegorm; his embarkation papers, with an excellent record of service, also state the date of the tragic sinking.
Photograph by Paolo Rossetti

gunners and four sailors had gone down with the *Thistlegorm*.

The Germans had made a lightening attack; the *Heinkel He 111s* had no trouble hitting at least one target since there were nearly twenty ships at anchor.

The second squadron of the 26th Kamp Geswader, stationed in Crete, was in action that night along the Sinai coast: in the light of a full moon the German pilots spotted the convoy and decided to attack the ship which appeared to be carrying the biggest cargo. They probably had no idea of the importance of the freighter they made their target. The gunners on the British ship had not even had time to load the cannon when the bombs dropped by the *Heinkels* hit the vessel right by No. 4 hold.

The *Thistlegorm* - newest of the Albyn Line's ships - was carrying a precious cargo of munitions and supplies for the British Eighth Army, engaged at that time in Operation Crusade, a major offensive launched by Montgomery and his men against the troops of General Rommel. Stacked in its holds were huge quantities of munitions and an assortment of military vehicles: *Bedford* trucks, *Morris* cars, *BSA* model *WDM20* motorbikes, plus endless boxes of *Lee-Enfield* rifles, spare parts, generators, Wellington boots, camp-beds and boxes of medical supplies. Stowed in Nos. 3 and 4 holds was a huge arsenal of explosives: anti-tank mines, artillery shells, boxed light munitions and hand grenades. Amid the great freighter's structures on the deck, together with the two paravanes (torpedo-shaped protective devices towed at the sides of the ship in mined areas to sever the moorings of contact mines), were two small tanks, four railway wagons and two railway engines. It was the colossal weight of its cargo that caused the *Thistlegorm* to sink so fast: the explosive in No. 4 hold tore the hull apart and the ship very quickly disappeared beneath the waves, dropping - still upright - onto the seabed". In 1956 Cousteau came to the Red Sea with the *Calypso*, on one of the exploratory missions that made such an important contribution to the advancement of scuba-diving the world over. The crew had no trouble finding the wreck: all the local fishermen knew of the great ship lying beneath the water and

E

F

D - The tragedy is still vividly recalled by Harry Bansall, whose first-person account of the events on these pages makes enthralling reading. Photograph by Paolo Rossetti

E - Plates and bottles, a porthole, even a tap, all memorabilia from the glorious wreck of the Thistlegorm. Photograph by Kurt Amsler

F - The engine-room telegraph has been recovered from the interior of the bridge; made of bronze, it has withstood its many years of immersion in salt water extremely well. Photograph by Kurt Amsler

A

B

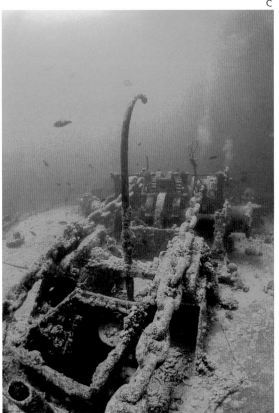

C

the huge fish that populated it. When they descended to the vessel, the French oceanographer and his men found it practically intact: masts, rigging, cargo handling booms, everything was still in place, as though the ship were merely sleeping. Thanks to Cousteau's film "The Silent World" and the extensive documentation he put together, the general public also got to know about the wreck of the *Thistlegorm* and experienced some of its magic and mystery. Although the fifty years spent on the bottom of the sea have taken their toll, the fascination of this huge freighter - crammed with all the supplies World War Two armies could have been in need of - has in no way diminished.

D

E

A - The wreck lies on the seabed, at 31 metres, slightly inclined on its port flank; in this picture a diver is seen approaching the huge structure of the stern.
Photograph by Roberto Rinaldi

B - The bow of the British cargo appears well-preserved, with the massive port anchor hanging from the hawsehole.
Photograph by Kurt Amsler

C - This picture shows the anchor winch, close to the bow; the fact that the starboard anchor is firmly dug into the bottom 60 metres from the wreck indicates that the Thistlegorm *was riding at anchor when she was bombed.*
Photograph by Paolo Rossetti

D - The huge, ghostly prow of the Thistlegorm *stands out against the infinite blue sea which has held it in its inclement grasp since the tragic night of October 5, 1941.*
Photograph by Kurt Amsler

E - Perhaps due to the dramatic circumstances of the Thistlegorm's *sinking or the outstanding historical interest of its cargo, this wreck is the best known in the Red Sea.*
Photograph by Kurt Amsler

F - Distinctly visible on the quarterdeck is the outline of the 120 mm cannon; the Luftwaffe air attack during the night of October 5-6, 1940 was so totally unexpected that the gunners on the British ship did not manage to fire a single cannon-shot. Photograph by Paolo Rossetti

G - Loaded on the deck were also four railway wagons, two of them probably used to transport the fuel needed by the ground forces engaged in fighting General Rommel's Afrika Korps. Photograph by Kurt Amsler

I

F

G

H

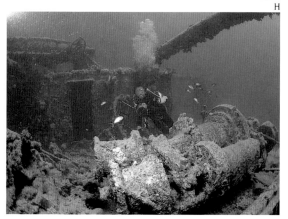

Diving to the wreck

The *Thistlegorm* lies in the stretch of sea between the Sha'al Ali reef and the west coast of Sinai, north of Ras Mohammed, in the Strait of Gobal. There are no visual points of reference: all that can be seen from here are the coast, far away to the east, and a few oil rigs to the north. The exact site of the wreck can therefore be identified only with the aid of a ship's instruments (GPS and sonic depth finder). The guide usually moors the boat by tying a cable to one of the huge structures on the main deck; it is therefore sensible to approach the vessel about halfway along its length. During dives it is extremely important to follow a number of safety measures. First of all, the descent and ascent must be made holding firmly onto the cable: the currents in this stretch of sea are sometimes very strong and changeable; it can happen that the current takes you in one direction on the surface and in the opposite direction when you are at depth.

H - At the foot of the foremast, now lying on its side, are the large winches used to manoeuvre the derricks. Photograph by Andrea and Antonella Ferrari

I - The structures of the bridge deck are still practically intact; some of the metal plating has given way but it is possible to enter both the bridge and the captain's cabin. Visible in this picture, behind the diver, is one of the lifeboat davits. Photograph by Paolo Rossetti

A

D - During dives to this huge wreck close attention must be paid to currents and safety rules - particularly regarding air supply - strictly followed.
Photograph by Roberto Rinaldi

E - An air duct can still be made out close to the companionway leading up to the bridge.
Photograph by Roberto Rinaldi

A - Among the many species to take advantage of the shelter offered by the wreck anthias and parrotfish are two of those most frequently encountered.
Photograph by Roberto Rinaldi

B - During the first dive and exploration of the wreck it is recommended starting from the main deck and leaving the interior of the holds and their finds until later.
Photograph by Kurt Amsler

C - Adorning a bitt are alcyonarians in a stunning shade of red; the entire wreck of the Thistlegorm has now been taken over by flourishing concretions of soft and hard corals.
Photograph by Roberto Rinaldi

B

C

D

E

F

F - Highlighted in the beam from a diver's torch is one of the two paravanes situated on the deck: these torpedo-like devices were used to remove mines from the waters immediately around the ship.
Photograph by Kurt Amsler

Another important precaution: when the air supply of the first diver in the group reaches 80 bar, start to return to the cable for the ascent, since this is a typical dive at the limit of the safety curve and air supply. Even if you encounter a strong current, one side of the ship is still sheltered: you can therefore plan each dive so that you start your exploration on this side, and are moving with, rather than against the current on the way back. It is difficult to say how many dives are needed to explore the wreck completely: there are so many thrilling things to see that nobody ever wants to leave the wreck behind. Personally I think it's worth making at least four dives. During the first you can take a thorough look at the main deck, at a depth of 18 metres. Finning your way along the promenade decks to both port and starboard, you encounter numerous now well-established coral formations and some members of the underwater community that has made the wreck its permanent home: groupers, twinspot snappers and angelfish, all specimens of an impressive size. As you move towards the bows, "flying" over the gigantic holds, you see the railway wagons, which probably contained coal; close by, on either side of the deck, are the paravanes. Continuing in this direction you reach the structures of the bow section, with the anchor winches and the chains emerging from the hawseholes. The port anchor is still hanging there; on the starboard side a long stretch of chain instead drops vertically to the seabed, at a depth of 31 metres, and then winds its way northwards to the anchor, 60 metres away: unmistakable evidence that the ship was anchored when it was bombed and sunk. Luxuriant coral growths make the vertically hanging chain a splendid subject for photographs. If you descend to the seabed and follow the chain a few metres, you get a real idea of just how huge a 9,000 ton freighter is. Back up at the bows it is time to start making your way back, on

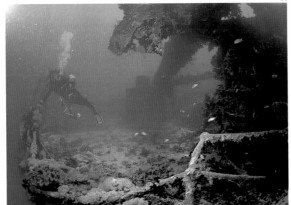

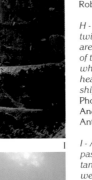

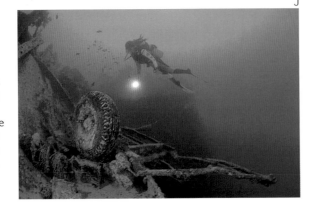

G - Collected together in a corner of one of the holds is a pile of rubber soles and tyres.
Photograph by Roberto Rinaldi

H - Torn and twisted plates are stark evidence of the explosion which split the heavy British cargo ship in two.
Photograph by Andrea and Antonella Ferrari

I - A diver swims past one of the two tank wagons which were being transported on deck.
Photograph by Kurt Amsler

J - Stacked in the holds of the Thistlegorm, as well as motorbikes, cars and other vehicles, were a number of trolleys for various uses, such as ground transportation of aerial bombs.
Photograph by Roberto Rinaldi

the opposite side, finning over the holds again (you will explore them during your second dive). Easily located along the promenade deck is what remains of Captain Ellis's quarters, the only ones with "en-suite" lavatory and bathtub. A short way further along is the entrance to a large room which was the canteen: towering over the scene is a radiator, now left hanging from its pipes. Beside it is the hatchway leading to the storeroom: I suggest you just look in rather than go right inside; it is a small space where there is little room to move and it is easy to kick up clouds of sediment. Nos. 1 and 2 holds are the objective of the second dive.

As soon as you descend through the wide opening of the first forward hold, you see that the cargo was loaded on two levels: deeper down there are still boxes of Lee-Enfield Mk3 rifles in racks of 10, boxes of medical supplies, camp-beds for field hospitals, aeroplane parts, mobile generators and some of the countless pairs above-the-knee rubber boots with which the holds were packed. On the upper level, still neatly lined up, are the Morris cars, with their spare tyre on the side. Practically nothing is now left of the engines and the dashboards too have been ransacked by uncivilized, selfish scuba divers who have done far greater damage than the water: on some vehicles

A - Stowed on board the Thistlegorm, together with the motor vehicles, were large quantities of spare parts and tyres; the tyres have been practically unaffected by the corrosive action of salt water.
Photograph by Roberto Rinaldi

B - A diver takes a close look at a Wellington boot, one of the many pairs included in the military supplies stacked on board, destined for the armed forces under the command of Field Marshal Montgomery.
Photograph by Roberto Rinaldi

C - Pictured here one of the boxes Lee-Enfield Mk3 rifles, still in their leather holders.
Photograph by Roberto Rinaldi

37

38

vever, you can still see the
r-stick, steering-wheel, pedals,
rview mirrors and windscreen.
e motorbikes nearby also have
nerous parts missing: many are
hout their headlamp or even
ir entire handlebars, pointlessly
pped off by ignorant trophy-
ters. Almost all the
torcycles are the *BSA WDM20*
del, manufactured specially for
itary use and particularly for
dispatch-riders corps which
ed the front with command
sts in the rear zone. In the very
pest part of no. 2 hold are
nerous trucks on which tens
d tens of these motorbikes were
sported. This area has suffered
st from plundering, partly
ause it is the most cramped
d dark to explore. Do not
ture in without an expert guide
, above all, without first
ecting the conditions of the
ks above: right on top of the
nt where you enter this hold
the goods wagons; their weight
already caused part of the
in deck to give way, and it is
steeply inclined towards the
left-hand corner. After taking
ng break on the surface, divers
ready for the third descent, to
lore the stern. When the ship
k after the explosion it was in
pieces; the stern is now tipped
r onto its port flank, no more
n 15 metres from the rest of the
sel. Start from the huge
peller and take time to admire

D

E

F

G

E - The Thistlegorm *was also transporting two light tanks, known as Bren-carriers since they were usually armed with one or two Bren machine-guns; one of the tanks can be clearly seen in this photo, lying on its side.*
Photograph by Andrea and Antonella Ferrari

F - A diver illuminates the front of a Morris *car; visible on the right are the rear axles of a* Bedford *truck.*
Photograph by Roberto Rinaldi

G - The row of Bedford *trucks still standing side by side at the bottom of No. 2 hold have a disturbingly spooky look about them.*
Photograph by Paolo Rossetti

D - The holds of this great cargo ship are an inexhaustible source of thrilling surprises and discoveries. Though many objects and furnishings have been removed by the first divers who visited the wreck, the Thistlegorm *and its load allow the reconstruction of an important page of history.*
Photograph by Roberto Rinaldi

the huge stern from its underside.
Many pieces of the ship were flung
in different directions by the
explosion and are still scattered all
around. Finning along the port
side you can go up to the after
bridge where the huge cannon and
anti-aircraft gun are now encrusted
with soft corals in an infinite
variety of colours.
For photographers this is perhaps
the most interesting area: as you
move among the pieces of
artillery, you will - with luck - have
close encounters with the many
groupers and snappers which,
with the southerly current, hover
practically motionless in the water.
Immediately below the main deck
you can continue along what is left
of the promenade deck, peering
from the portholes into the
gunners' cabins and through
the rudder inspection hatch.
The main objective of the fourth
dive is one of the two railway
engines loaded on the deck above
No. 4 hold; it was catapulted by
the explosion to a spot about 20
metres from the ship. Starting
from the point where the ship was
torn apart, on the port side, move
westwards: after just a few metres,
you will see the engine, its wheels
resting on the seabed, instantly
recognizable from the classic,
cylindrical shape of its boiler and
the front buffers. Its smokestack
has disappeared and the water
inside the boiler teems with
thousands of glassfish which have

A

B

C

A - In this archive photo taken shortly before the beginning of the war, an instructor watches a recruit learning to ride a BSA *motorbike very similar to the ones stowed on board the* Thistlegorm.
Photograph by Paolo Rossetti

B - Now totally smothered by encrusting organisms, the BSA *motorbikes lie side by side in the first forward hold.*
Photograph by Roberto Rinaldi

C - When exploring the holds great care must be taken not to kick up sediment which would seriously reduce visibility.
Photograph by Andrea and Antonella Ferrari

made this tortuous place their home, like the groupers, crocodilefish and scorpionfish you have every chance of meeting. The huge metal wheels of the locomotive are decked with multi-coloured alcyonarians, like garlands: even a whole roll of film would not be wasted here. The last part of the dive before your ascent can be spent back on the wreck, exploring the mass of ammunition and supplies thrown from the hold when it was ripped open by the explosion: huge piles of explosives, bombs and arms, mixed up with remains of the trucks they were being transported on. Also here, almost intact, are two light military tanks,

F

G

D

H

E

known as tankettes, over which angelfish now stand guard. As you make your ascent, remember to take nothing but photographs and mental pictures with you. This cargo boat is now a monument to a war which left behind thousands of wrecks like this one and the greatest respect must be shown for the five gunners and four sailors of the *Thistlegorm* who, like thousands of others, now rest in peace in a watery grave.

E - A diver examines the rear tyres of a large Bedford truck: these vehicles were used both to transport troops and carry ammunition. Photograph by Roberto Rinaldi

F - In desert warfare motorbikes played a vital role in keeping the various parts of the front in contact with one another; all the field forces had special units of despatch riders. Clearly visible in this photograph is the front fork with link suspensions. Photograph by Andrea and Antonella Ferrari

G - On the upper level of No. 1 hold the remains of the Morris cars are still a splendid sight; they were presumably intended for use by British officers during the North-African campaign. Photograph by Roberto Rinaldi

H - On the upper level of No. 1 hold are the superb remains of the Morris cars; features to note are the spare wheel on the right-hand side and the pattern of corrugations on the tyre tread, particularly suited to driving on sandy desert tracks. The front headlights are of the kind typically mounted on vehicles used in war zones. Photograph by Roberto Rinaldi

D - Thoughtless trophy-hunters have made the Morris cars the main target of their souvenir grabbing raids. Photograph by Roberto Rinaldi

THE CARGO BOAT AT GOBAL SHAGHIR
by Roberto Rinaldi

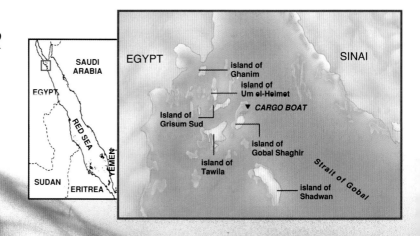

RATINGS

Finding site: easy.
Visibility: fairly good.
Current: often very strong.
Dive difficulty: medium to difficult.
Presence of lines or nets: none.
Historical interest: low.
Photographic interest: medium.
Biological interest: high.

DATA FILE

Type of wreck: cargo ship.
Nationality: unknown.
Year of construction: unknown.
Tonnage: unknown.
Date of sinking: unknown.
Cause of sinking: collision with reef.
Site position: reef north of Gobal
        Shaghir, not far from Bluff
        Point lighthouse.
Distance from shore: against the
        reef.
Minimum depth: 5 metres.
Maximum depth: 25 metres.

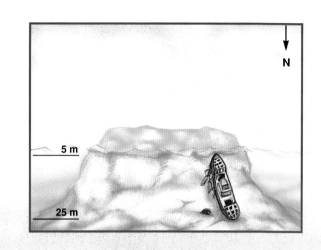

THE CARGO BOAT AT GOBAL SHAGHIR

A few hundred metres from the Bluff Point lighthouse is another wreck, in this case a fairly large vessel which sank a century ago after colliding with the reef on the northern edge of the island of Gobal Shaghir. Unlike the "mini-wreck", not too far from here, this British merchant ship, apparently with a cargo of electrical material, is located on a coral barrier facing north, a site particularly exposed to the prevailing wind and often to forceful currents. Although the wreck does not lie at great depth - its bow at 5-6 metres, its stern at 25 metres - in certain wind and sea conditions the dive can be tricky.

Diving to the wreck

Before plunging into these waters you should therefore wait for a day when weather conditions are good; your patience will be amply rewarded by the beauty of the underwater environment awaiting you beneath the surface. No dive to the wreck would be complete without a thorough exploration of the densely populated coral reef of which it is now an integral part. Rather than head straight for the wreck, your guide will therefore lead you some 20-30 metres further on, to its east or west depending on the current.
Let the flow of the water carry you along the coral drop-off with its lush profusion of lifeforms, as far as the huge stern, lying intact at a depth of 25 metres. Half of the large four-bladed screw emerges from the sea floor and it is thickly clad with the alcyonarians typical of tropical waters. The entire stern section of the hull is colonized by the *Tubastrea*, a cynidarian with pinkish calyxes, not unlike the *Astroides* found in the southern Mediterranean which waits until dark to open its yellow corolla of tentacles. This part of the ship is the most intact, and on the deck too you can still make out specific

A - The distinctive bright orange colour of the anthias makes it an eye-catching presence among the extensively encrusted structures of the British merchant ship; the vessel went down - probably at the end of the last century - only a few hundred metres from Bluff Point lighthouse, on the north coast of the island of Gobal Shaghir. Photograph by Roberto Rinaldi

B - Resting on the seabed at a depth of 25 metres, the stern is the best-conserved part of the vessel: one can still make out the shapes of several bitts and the uprights of the railings. Photograph by Roberto Rinaldi

structures of the old vessel. Further along its length, the desk and flanks are instead in a much deteriorated state and there are gaping holes through which you can enter what were once the ship's holds. Part of the cargo can still be seen here: mainly electrical material, porcelain insulators, old batteries. Inside the holds there are also two handsome branches of black coral, a particular feature of this wreck. Some 20-30 metres away, in the direction of Bluff Point, are a series of structures that got separated from the ship: a large wheel whose purpose is unclear and a group of metal plates, now home to a dense

school of glass-fish. Be on your guard while exploring around here: concealed amongst the iron plating and coral are probably some incredibly well-camouflaged, highly poisonous stonefish. Keep your eyes on the seafloor, watching for the eyes or mouth which alone might betray their brilliant camouflage. But glass-fish and stonefish are certainly not the only fish to be seen in and around this wreck. At a site like this - facing the open sea and swept by strong currents - nothing could be more normal than to encounter large shoals of jacks, occasional sharks and, especially, huge groupers which can frequently be spotted amidst the coral and the wreck.

E

F

G

C - Soft corals and concretions formed by other organisms entirely cover the still exposed parts of the rudder and huge screw (both have partly sunk into the sandy sea floor).
Photograph by Roberto Rinaldi

D - A dense shoal of glassfish passes beneath a handsome sea fan which has settled on a metal structure lying a few metres from the ship's hull.
Photograph by Roberto Rinaldi

E - This huge metal wheel - its function still unknown - can be seen some twenty metres or so from the wreck; on the right-hand side of the picture is a fine looking scorpionfish hovering close to the seabed.
Photograph by Roberto Rinaldi

F - Some of the structures of the British merchant ship are still in a perfect state of conservation; going by its design, it was built in the second half of the 19th century. Still tied to the bitt pictured here is a thick hemp rope.
Photograph by Roberto Rinaldi

G - In the ship's interior, amid the collapsed remains of the living quarters, one can still make out the shape of a bathtub, now covered in rust and concretions; when moving about among the debris, a careful watch must be kept for stonefish with their sometimes fatal poison.
Photograph by Andrea Ghisotti

49

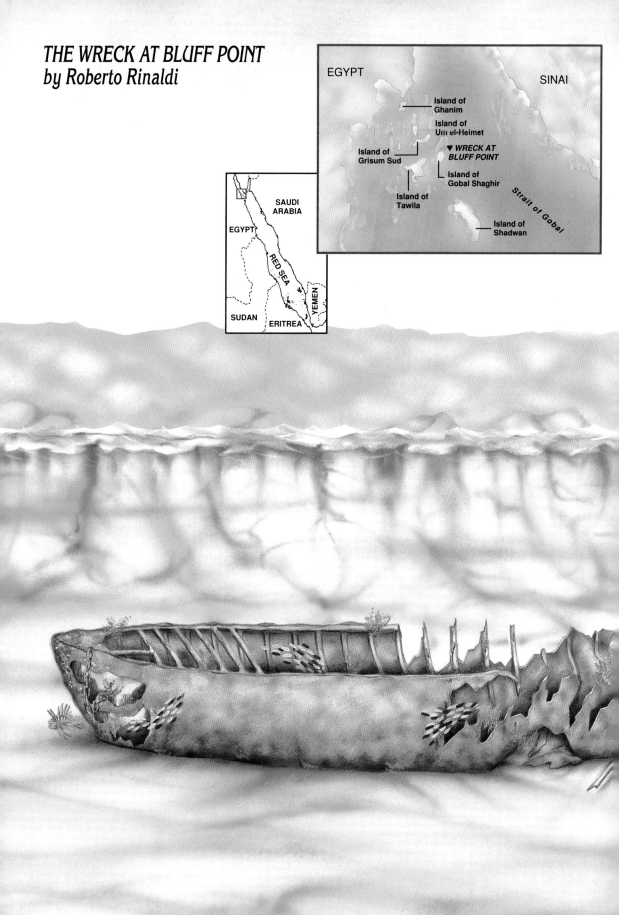

THE WRECK AT BLUFF POINT
by Roberto Rinaldi

EGYPT

SINAI

Island of
Ghanim

Island of
Um el-Heimet

Island of
Grisum Sud

▼ WRECK AT
BLUFF POINT

Island of
Gobal Shaghir

Island of
Tawila

Strait of Gobal

Island of
Shadwan

SAUDI
ARABIA

EGYPT

RED SEA

SUDAN

ERITREA

YEMEN

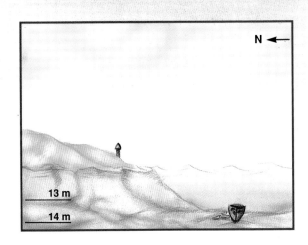

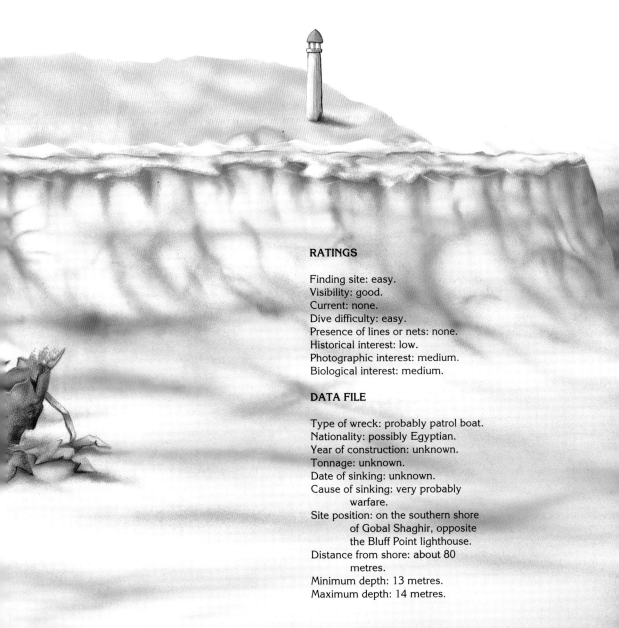

RATINGS

Finding site: easy.
Visibility: good.
Current: none.
Dive difficulty: easy.
Presence of lines or nets: none.
Historical interest: low.
Photographic interest: medium.
Biological interest: medium.

DATA FILE

Type of wreck: probably patrol boat.
Nationality: possibly Egyptian.
Year of construction: unknown.
Tonnage: unknown.
Date of sinking: unknown.
Cause of sinking: very probably
        warfare.
Site position: on the southern shore
        of Gobal Shaghir, opposite
        the Bluff Point lighthouse.
Distance from shore: about 80
        metres.
Minimum depth: 13 metres.
Maximum depth: 14 metres.

THE MINI-WRECK AT BLUFF POINT

Little is known about the "mini-wreck" located at Bluff Point. The tale considered most plausible by captains of local cruise boats is that it was an Egyptian gunboat which sank for unknown reasons during the war with Israel. The wreck itself is now no more than a skeleton, about 20 metres long, resting on the sandy bottom and offering few clues to its exact identity. Although the remains of the vessel are of little historical interest or visual impact, the Bluff Point wreck has become very popular with divers. This is partly due to its "strategic" position: it lies in the shallow water of a bay well-protected from the north-west winds, often used as an overnight mooring by cruise boats.
Its popularity is also due to the surprising abundance of spectacular underwater organisms - of special interest to photographers - which have made their home amid the plates of the wreck, the only hard surface to be found on the sandy seafloor stretching for miles around.

Diving to the wreck

The sunken ship is close to the southern shore of the small island of Gobal Shaghir, which continues south-west and practically touches the eastern edge of its elder sister island: Gobal Kebir. At low tide the two rocky outcrops become one, linked by a narrow strip of white sand, an ideal place to relax for a few hours. The tiny lighthouse on the north-east tip of Gobal Shaghir, Bluff Point, seems to have been put there with the very purpose of indicating the best position to moor and the site of the wreck. Wonderful dives can be made starting from the point and continuing westwards, where the vertical coral wall drops to a depth of more than 30 metres and offers an incredible variety of underwater life. In the bay itself the water is instead shallow: the wreck lies on the sand at 14 metres, an ideal

B

A - A diver observes the "mini-wreck" - as it is called - lies at a depth of 14 metres just a short way from the Bluff Point lighthouse, on the tiny island of Gobal Shaghir. Although nothing definite is known about the origins of the wreck, it is probably the remains of an Egyptian gunboat, sunk by the Israelis at the time of the war of Yom Kippur or, even more likely, during the Six-Day War of 1967. Photograph by Alberto Muro

B - The dive to the wreck at Bluff Point is fairly easy and can be recommended for all divers, irrespective of their experience. The best place to moor is close to the lighthouse. From here the vessel is simple to locate: descending along the coral wall directly below and swimming westwards, the shape of the ship soon comes into view against the expanse of white sand. Photograph by Alberto Muro

depth for a carefree dive, and for an enjoyable night dive too. Make your descent along the short coral ridge right below the lighthouse and, keeping a certain distance away from the ridge, swim westwards until you spot the boat, its shape well-defined against the white sand. The structures of the vessel have been completely destroyed but it is still in an upright position, its metal main and bulkhead frames intact.

Make your way straight to the stern, which is still reasonably well conserved; adorned with colourful soft corals, it is undoubtedly the most stunning and photogenic part of the vessel, and you'll get some outstanding pictures of the underwater habitat here.

But the subject most likely to catch photographers' attention is the dense shoal of silver glass-fish which stations almost permanently in the wreck. Large turkeyfish swim to and fro in their midst, beneath a glaring sun visible through the clear water. An exceptional place, therefore, to try to take some memorable souvenir pictures of the visual feast offered by the Red Sea. At night the wreck looks totally different. Make sure you have a macro lens to obtain some good close-up shots, for example of the many slate-pencil sea urchins or poisonous red urchins; you may even encounter the *Astrosparthus* which during the night spreads out its countless arms to the current to trap suspended particles of plankton. But perhaps the most sought-after subjects for nighttime close-ups are the so-called "Spanish dancers", not infrequently seen around these parts after dark. They are large, bright-red nudibranchs which propel themselves through the water with rhythmic contractions of their body, bringing to mind the swirling skirts of a flamenco dancer.

C

D

C - All that is left of the wreck is the skeleton of the hull, covered by a magnificent assortment of corals in colours ranging from delicate to garish; this breathtaking spectacle alone makes the dive worthwhile.
Photograph by Alberto Muro

D - The unmistakable profile of a giant grouper appears from behind a clump of coral growing on the rusty girders of the wreck.
Photograph by Roberto Rinaldi

E - Here as in every wreck gleaming glassfish dart to and fro, a spectacular but commonplace sight in the fascinating underwater world of the Red Sea.
Photograph by Roberto Rinaldi

E

GHIANNIS D.
by Andrea Ghisotti

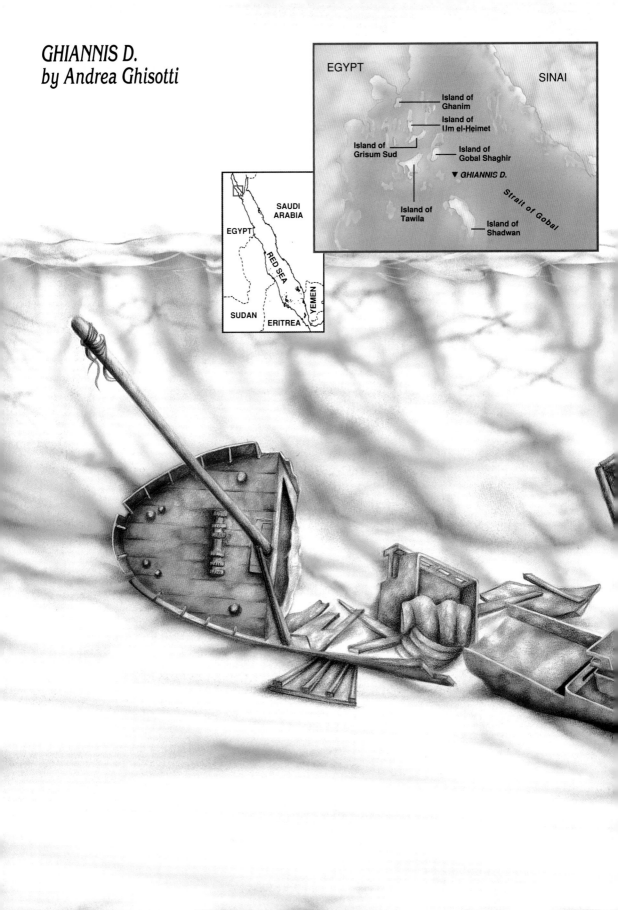

EGYPT

SINAI

Island of
Ghanim

Island of
Um el-Heimet

Island of
Grisum Sud

Island of
Gobal Shaghir

▼ GHIANNIS D.

Strait of Gobal

Island of
Tawila

Island of
Shadwan

SAUDI
ARABIA

EGYPT

RED SEA

SUDAN

ERITREA

YEMEN

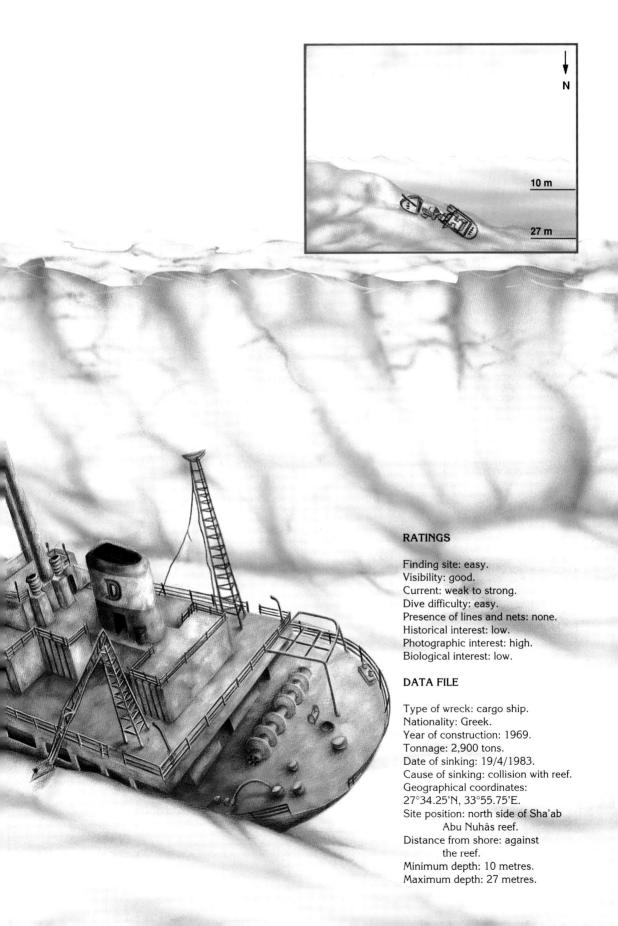

RATINGS

Finding site: easy.
Visibility: good.
Current: weak to strong.
Dive difficulty: easy.
Presence of lines and nets: none.
Historical interest: low.
Photographic interest: high.
Biological interest: low.

DATA FILE

Type of wreck: cargo ship.
Nationality: Greek.
Year of construction: 1969.
Tonnage: 2,900 tons.
Date of sinking: 19/4/1983.
Cause of sinking: collision with reef.
Geographical coordinates:
27°34.25'N, 33°55.75'E.
Site position: north side of Sha'ab
　　　Abu Nuhâs reef.
Distance from shore: against
　　　the reef.
Minimum depth: 10 metres.
Maximum depth: 27 metres.

THE CARGO BOAT
GHIANNIS D.

It is not hard to find an explanation for the shipwreck of the *Carnatic*: instrumentation at the time was far from sophisticated and the efficiency of the elementary propulsion systems installed left much to be desired.
But what about the *Ghiannis D.*? Why this modern cargo boat should have sunk little more than ten years ago, right beside the old British vessel, is indeed puzzling. But mystification turns to amazement on learning that there are other modern ships lying close to these two. It is as though a curse had been cast on the reef of Sha'ab Abu Nuhâs. How can it be that even today big ships fall prey to navigation errors and currents? The tale of the *Ghiannis D.* is not unlike many other stories of the Red Sea. The ship was a 2,900 ton freighter, many times bought and sold, which may have begun its life in a Japanese shipyard which launched it as the *Shoyo Maru*: this is the name that appeared on the bow, once old layers of paint had worn away. And the seemingly Greek name *Marcos* has also appeared, on top of it. But not even this was the name of the ship at the time it sank: when it hit the rocks of Abu Nuhâs on April 19, 1983 it sailed under the Greek flag and was called *Ghiannis*. The "D" tagged on the end of its name simply indicated the shipping line, Danae. No mystery either about its port of departure, and its destination: it had set out from Rijeka and was heading for Hodeida, on the Yemeni coast of the southern Red Sea. The vessel was about a hundred metres long (99 metres, to be precise) and had two engines with two propeller shafts, a much more effective system than one central propeller when changing direction. But even this was not enough to save it. No lives were lost, however, as the ship remained afloat for six weeks before the force of the sea split her in two and the stern slipped to a

A - The stern of the Ghiannis D. *lies on the seabed at a depth between 23 and 27 metres, tilted on its port side; battered by the waves, the vessel - about 100 metres in length - broke in two a few weeks after its shipwreck.*
Photograph by Vincenzo Paolillo

B - *Not quite so deep down (at around 18 metres), the bow is exceptionally well preserved; like the stern, it is resting on its port flank; in this photo the anchor chain can be seen stretching down from the starboard hawsehole.*
Photograph by Kurt Amsler

depth of 23-27 metres. For a long time the bow remained above water, indicating the position of the ship; but it eventually sank onto the reef below, collapsing on its left flank.

Diving to the wreck

Although the wreck of the *Ghiannis D.* is not old, it is very interesting and exceptionally photogenic, a paradise for underwater photography buffs. The dive cannot be made any time: when seas in the Strait of Gobal are stormy, the current has such force that it has dug what can only be described as craters

C

D

E

C - On the quarterdeck are several bitts, a huge winch and metal poles which once held up a canvas awning; all of them, and the railing too, are still intact. On the latter, numerous stony coral formations stand out.
Photograph by Vincenzo Paolillo

D - It is only ten years since the Ghiannis D. *sank but in many parts of the wreck splendid soft corals in assorted colours already grow in lush profusion, often to an amazing size.*
Photograph by Alberto Muro

E - Although inclined at a sharp angle, the forward mast has withstood the plunge to the seabed and the force of the currents; still firmly in position, its wind-braces continue to do their job, avoiding the mast to fall on the seabed.
Photograph by Vincenzo Paolillo

F - Minute life forms carried by the currents provide a constant source of nourishment for the flourishing soft corals which lavishly adorn the wreck, heightening its spectacular impact.
Photograph by Kurt Amsler

F

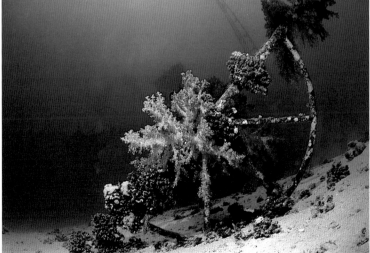

A

A - Prominent on both sides of the large funnel, still standing on the bridge deck, is the letter "D", the initial of the Greek shipping line, Danae.
Photograph by Andrea Ghisotti

B - The structures on the quarterdeck are still in an excellent condition; visible in this picture, on either side of the mast, are two large air ducts which communicated with the engine room below.
Photograph by Andrea Ghisotti

C - This photograph highlights the section of the stern, a stunning sight with its structures wrapped in multi-coloured corals and yet each single part still clearly recognizable.
Photograph by Roberto Rinaldi

D - A diver hovers over the stern section, illuminating the hard coral concretions which now decorate the entire wreck.
Photograph by Kurt Amsler

E, F - Moving incessantly this way and that among the superstructures, shoals of anthias create a kaleidoscope of reflections, in magical contrast to the solemn stillness of the wreck.
Photographs by Vincenzo Paolillo

G - On the Ghiannis D., as on many freighters which ply the waters of the Red Sea, the quarterdeck was protected from the sun by a huge awning, supported by a metal frame that is still visible on the wreck.
Photograph by Kurt Amsler

B

C

D

in the sandy seabed to the left of the stern - and at a depth of 25 metres, what's more!

But with a calm sea it is a wonderful dive, easy even for novices. You had best start your exploration from the stern, which is the deepest part, and gradually ascend towards the midships section and prow. The whole quarter-deck as far as the first hold is still in one piece: before you start exploring, it is worth finning a few metres seaward, away from the stern; from this point, floating midwater, you get an overview of half the ship and it is a truly spectacular sight, especially if the sun illuminates the starboard side.

The whole stern section is resting on its port side, but without listing too far over. You can therefore just see the starboard screw, its blades twisted by the impact.

Remain midwater for a moment or two: you will notice all sorts of details which might escape you when exploring in greater haste or from closer-up. Towering over the front of the quarter-deck is the funnel, with a large "D" on both sides.

In front of it is the bridge, behind are other rooms, a huge winch, the bitts and the railings, still intact and not even twisted, the same as the poles from which a canvas awning once hung over part of the quarterdeck.

The trellis which supported the booms used to load and unload cargo in the stern hold is now pointing towards the surface at an angle of 45°, likewise a mast situated behind the funnel, on the starboard side. All the structures of the vessel stretch high up into the water, and in fact come to within a few metres of the surface. Having made the most of this panoramic view, move closer to the ship and explore its individual features. At the foot of the funnel are the doors leading to the engine room, a kind of dark well into which only really expert divers who do not suffer from claustrophobia should venture. Access is actually not difficult but little light filters in and it is important to know the right way

E

to move around, so as not to stir up the mud which covers the structures. A good torch is obviously an essential item here. The engines are a splendid sight, with their long lines of rocker arms and springs, still fairly free of concretions.

The water here, as in every engine room, teems with tiny silver fish: hatchetfish and the more slender glass-fish. You get another fine view looking upwards through the open hatches, with the funnel illuminated by sunlight.

H - The anthias is one of the most common fish of the Red Sea, ever-present in and around wrecks: the holds and crevices between metal structures offer an ideal shelter for these decidedly sociable fish. Photograph by Roberto Rinaldi

F

I

G

H

Be careful as you leave: a giant moray has made its home here and, while harmless enough, does not appreciate having fins flipped across its snout!

The bridge and the other rooms in the stern of the vessel are now bare, stripped of instrumentation and other fixtures and furnishings that can make a visit interesting. Access to the holds is extremely easy but they are completely empty: the midships section is a total shambles, its plating torn-

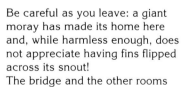

I - In spite of the thick encrustations and flourishing corals, it is still possible to make out the sprocket wheel and other mechanical parts of this winch. Photograph by Roberto Rinaldi

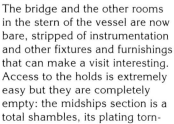

A

B

away and twisted, its flanks collapsed on the seabed.
This is a good place to observe crocodilefish and the ever-present scorpionfish although if you are taking photographs or shooting videos, the "walls" of silver fish - so solid they make your companions disappear momentarily from view - offer more stunning picture material. This part of the wreck also abounds in parrotfish which ignore divers and continue their non-stop nibbling of metal plates and stony coral, which they obviously find very tasty. The bow too is intact and worth examining: its tall mast is still in place but now parallel to the seafloor, since the bow has

A - A large parrotfish appears to be mesmerized by this rope which, caught up in some metal structure, sways gently with the current.
Photograph by Vincenzo Paolillo

B - The blades of the starboard screw appear to be completely crushed, indicating that the keel must have scraped along the reef while the engines were still operating at full throttle. Fortunately no lives were lost when the ship hit the reef; shortly after the collision all the men on board were rescued and taken to Shadwan.
Photograph by Kurt Amsler

C - As can be seen from this photograph, through the windows, some of the rooms have now collapsed and only the outer walls are still standing; it is therefore important to watch out for plates that may be unsafe.
Photograph by Vincenzo Paolillo

C

D

D - With the battering taken by the wreck in the weeks and months after it sank and the action of the salt water, the tiles which formerly covered large areas of walls and floors have become detached, and are now piled in the corners of the rooms.
Photograph by Roberto Rinaldi

E

E - The scene encountered in the midships section of the vessel speaks of total destruction and yet a hook still hangs in its proper position on the arm of a derrick, witnessing the tragic atmosphere that accompanies the dive to a wreck.
Photograph by Vincenzo Paolillo

F - Exploring the bridge, cabins, engine room and what is left of the holds makes the dive to the Ghiannis D. an enthralling experience.
Photograph by Vincenzo Paolillo

F

turned right over onto its port flank, at a depth of about 18 metres. Observing it from above you see the two names, *Marcos* and, just below, in smaller letters, *Shoyo Maru*. Maybe a third will appear in time!

Begin your ascent from the hawse-holes; the anchor chains provide a very convenient guide and, when making a decompression stop prior to surfacing, take a last look at the anchors, lowered during the frantic moments of the fatal collision with the reef.

G

I

H

G - Divers who venture into the dark engine room are bound to feel a thrill at the sight of the long rows of rocker arms, valves and springs, still fairly free of encrustation; space is tight here so it is important to move carefully, to avoid stirring up clouds of sediment.
Photograph by Andrea Ghisotti

H - When exploring the wreck it is not unusual to come across a *crocodilefish resting on the metal plating or partly buried in silt, well camouflaged while waiting for a hapless victim to come swimming past.*
Photograph by Sergio Quaglia

I - In this photograph a diver is seen exploring one of the accessible areas below deck. Before venturing inside a wrecked ship it is essential to locate possible ways out.
Photograph by Roberto Rinaldi

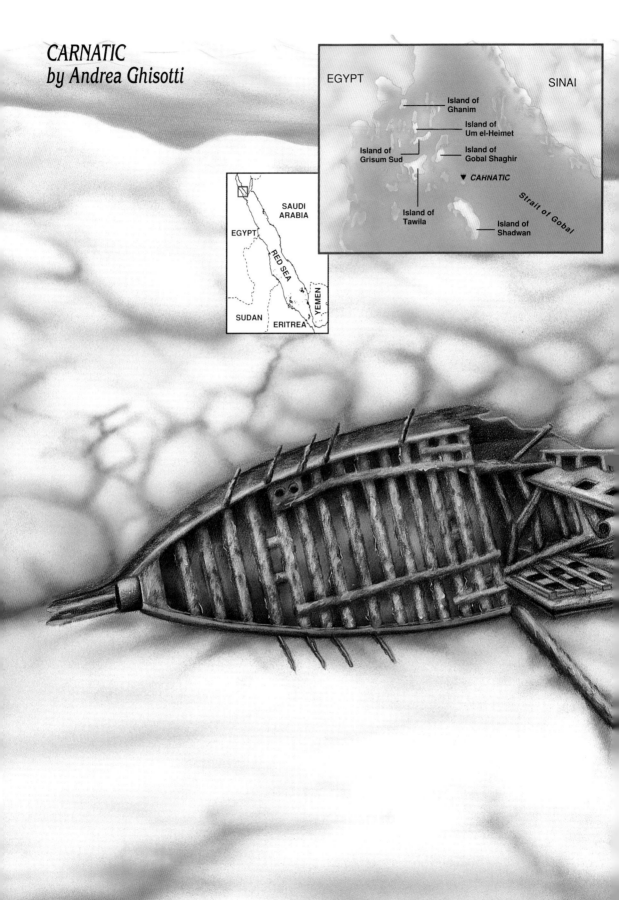

CARNATIC
by Andrea Ghisotti

EGYPT

SINAI

Island of
Ghanim

Island of
Um el-Heimet

Island of
Grisum Sud

Island of
Gobal Shaghir

▼ *CAHNATIC*

Strait of Gobal

Island of
Tawila

Island of
Shadwan

SAUDI
ARABIA

EGYPT

RED SEA

YEMEN

SUDAN

ERITREA

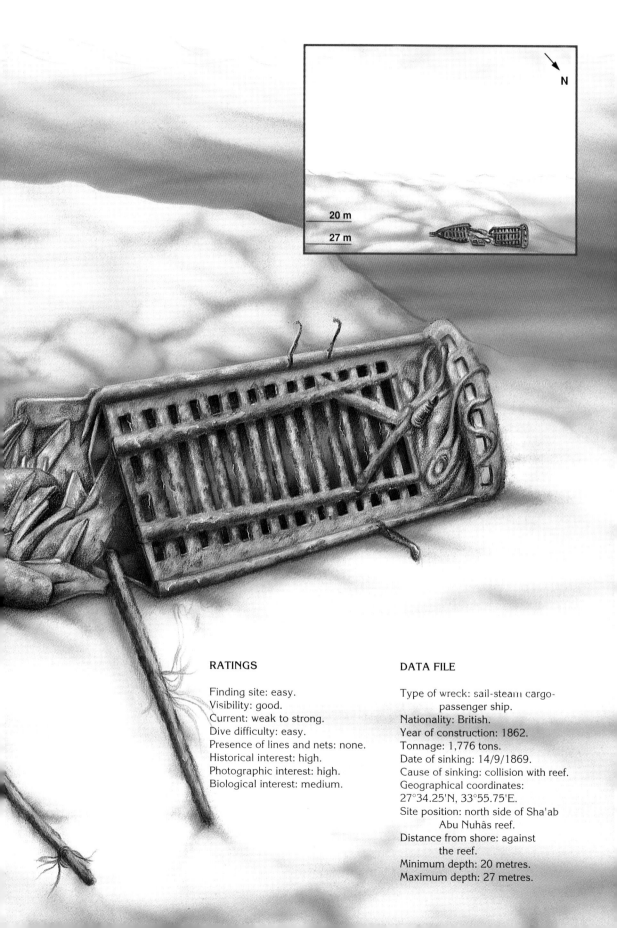

RATINGS

Finding site: easy.
Visibility: good.
Current: weak to strong.
Dive difficulty: easy.
Presence of lines and nets: none.
Historical interest: high.
Photographic interest: high.
Biological interest: medium.

DATA FILE

Type of wreck: sail-steam cargo-
    passenger ship.
Nationality: British.
Year of construction: 1862.
Tonnage: 1,776 tons.
Date of sinking: 14/9/1869.
Cause of sinking: collision with reef.
Geographical coordinates:
27°34.25'N, 33°55.75'E.
Site position: north side of Sha'ab
    Abu Nuhâs reef.
Distance from shore: against
    the reef.
Minimum depth: 20 metres.
Maximum depth: 27 metres.

THE STEAMER *CARNATIC*

A

The wreck of the *Carnatic* is one of the best known and most visited dive sites in the northern part of the Red Sea, easily reached by boat from Hurghada or, better still, when cruising on a live-aboard boat specially equipped for divers.
And yet whenever I hear the name, my heart misses a beat because I was one of the people (the others were Renzo, a close Italian friend, who was working on a charter boat in the area, and Mauro, an underwater diver on board one of the Italian mine-sweepers belonging to the Multinational Force and Observers stationed at Sharm el-Sheikh) who discovered the name and history of this sunken vessel after a long, tiring search that involved more excitement and suspense than many thrillers. Let me tell you the tale. It all started with two bottles of a distinctive double-curved shape, made from very thick, greenish glass. Renzo picked them up from the harbour bed where they had been thrown by Adrian, skipper of the Lady Jane V, because they were slightly broken. They had been found during a dive to a newly discovered, unknown sunken ship on the other side of the strait of Gobal. Renzo did not know the exact point but had a vague idea where the place was. Having decided to go and look for the wreck, we crossed the strait at dawn on a still spring morning with a calm sea and little wind (a rare thing around these parts).
After hugging the eastern shore of the island of Shadwan, we headed towards Sha'ab Abu Nuhâs: this reef is the last "barrier" on the edge of the Strait of Gobal and a menace to ships that ply these waters, since they find themselves in a narrow channel between this perilous reef and Beacon Rock, on the far side of the strait, in water that flows faster and faster, like a river in flood, creating eddying currents and violent waves.
And there is plenty of evidence of its perils: carcasses of modern

B

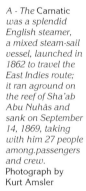

C

A - The Carnatic was a splendid English steamer, a mixed steam-sail vessel, launched in 1862 to travel the East Indies route; it ran aground on the reef of Sha'ab Abu Nuhâs and sank on September 14, 1869, taking with him 27 people among passengers and crew.
Photograph by Kurt Amsler

B - The ship's cargo included wine and "London soda water" contained in bottles of a double-curved shape, made from greenish opal-glass; it was the chance and providential finding of some of these bottles that made it possible to locate the wreck.
Photograph by Andrea Ghisotti

ships that have run aground and been broken up by the sea litter the whole eastern and northern sides of Abu Nuhâs. Renzo believed the wreck we were looking for would be on the side most exposed to the prevailing northerly winds, so we dropped anchor north of the reef. First to dive in, Renzo re-surfaced within minutes, shouting elatedly: "She's here, she's here, beautiful, huge, come on quickly!". I grabbed

my camera and plunged in after him, finning to the point indicated. On the sandy seabed at a depth of 25 metres, its profile first blurred and gradually sharper, the unmistakable form of an old ship came into view. Lying on its port flank, it had a strange tapered, slender shape, with a low, flattened poop, typical of a sailing ship. I descended a few more metres to get a better look at the stern and

C - Also the discovery of this piece of a plate made of Ironstone china helped give a name to the wreck.
Photograph by Andrea Ghisotti

D - The stern lies at a depth of 25 metres, leaning heavily on its port flank; its flattened, square shape is typical of traditional 19th century sailing vessels.
Photograph by Roberto Rinaldi

E - The lifeboat davits are still in place on both sides of the stern.
Photograph by Kurt Amsler

F - Resting on its port flank, the bow of the Carnatic is covered in a mantle of hard coral formations and magnificent alcyonarians; it is still possible to make out the point where the bowsprit used to go.
Photograph by Kurt Amsler

G - The combined destructive effects of shipworms and salt water have eaten away the wooden planking that covered the deck, leaving the metal framework of the vessel exposed.
Photograph by Kurt Amsler

D

E
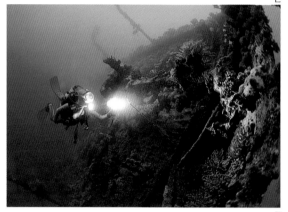

F
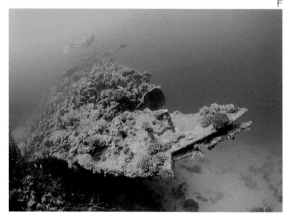

G

found the huge rudder resting on the bottom and the large three-bladed screw stuck in the sand and covered with soft corals. There could be no further doubt: it was a steam ship. And yet its shape did not convince me... The poop deck had lost its wooden planking, destroyed by shipworms and the passage of time, and it was easy to make my way inside, passing first one deck, then another before reaching the holds. Further ahead the midships section was a mass of contorted metal but I could still make out the huge boiler, part of the engines and the remains of the funnel. But an unexpected and thrilling surprise awaited me at the very bottom: two masts, with their rigging wrapped in the tight hold of stony coral. So I had not been mistaken after all: the wreck was that of a mixed steam-sail vessel, one of the stupendous hybrids built during the 19th century, when engines were taking over but sails were still able to achieve higher speeds, besides being a safety precaution. The stern section, also resting on its port side, was in a good condition and it was through here that I made my way to the hold, where my companions were searching excitedly. There were wooden cases, now in pieces, and endless wine bottles of assorted shapes and sizes, as well as a few unusual small curved bottles, like the ones picked up by the previous visitors to the wreck. I also came across a few broken pieces of plates and cups and took one I thought might help identify the wreck. The foredeck had also lost its planking and I could see its steel frame with, at the far end, the huge metal ring into which the bowsprit once fitted. Viewed from above the bow was a beautiful sight, long and slim like that of a clipper. Our air had finished and so had our adventure: the sea became rougher and no further dives were possible for a while. The wreck therefore had to be identified with the few clues we had obtained, a challenging and arduous task. A few of the little bottles had "Calcutta" or "Bombay" in relief on the glass, others the words "Soda Water". The city name was

A

B

A - Here several divers are pictured hovering over the bow of the Carnatic; the ship is now one of the best known wrecks and most popular dives of the whole Red Sea.
Photograph by Massimo Bicciato

B - Thick clumps of soft corals have developed in certain parts of the wreck, some of them growing to a truly amazing size.
Photograph by Vincenzo Paolillo

C - Now partly sunk into the sand, the rudder and three-blade screw still appear to be well preserved.
Photograph by Vincenzo Paolillo

D - A diver swims inside the poop deck, along what is left of the first-class deck; here too the wooden planking has almost completely disappeared.
Photograph by Andrea Ghisotti

probably their intended destination. In all likelihood the ship was therefore an English one, bound for colonies in India. The wine bottles were instead marked with a large no.2, again in relief on the glass. As for the ship, its shape classified it as one of the first mixed steam-sail vessels, very similar to the *Rhône*, a splendid sunken ship which went down in the British Virgin Islands. The *Rhône* was built in 1865; our ship must have been built around the same time.
Back in Italy I involved my mother in the search. A pioneer scuba diver, she too became passionately interested in the wreck and waded determinedly through endless volumes of Lloyd's register books, making long lists of possible shipwrecks. It was only during this stage of our research that I realized just how many ships and lives have been lost in the Red Sea: hundreds and hundreds of vessels, many of them gone without trace, others leaving only very basic data on the date and place of the shipwreck, others still - but a minority - with a few lines that sum up a tremendous drama at sea. I busied myself trying to decipher some writing which, once the encrustations had been removed, appeared on the piece of broken plate picked up in the hold.
Of the three words incised one on top of the other, only one was legible: "Real". Even with a binocular microscope I could not decipher the other two words,

C

D

so I tried with photography; I took a picture of the writing using a high-definition film and very strong lighting and then projected the words onto a large screen.
And sure enough, it was possible to decipher something more. The third word was "China", the second ended in "... stone". Consulting books on pottery and chinaware in 19th century Britain, we discovered that "Ironstone China" is a hardwearing type of China made by adding glassy ironstone slag to the usual porcelain constituents: this makes it very tough and extremely similar to porcelain, though less shiny. The system was invented and patented by Charles J. Mason in 1813 and the china produced exclusively in his factory until

1827. He then licensed the process to other factories: one, called Longport, was a well-established maker of good quality, low-cost chinawares and supplied most of the china used on board British ships. The Longport factory closed in 1876, however, which presumably meant that our ship had been fitted out before that year, even if it sank later. While staying in the Red Sea we had visited the wreck of another mixed steam-sail vessel which sank at Beacon Rock, on the other side of the Strait of Gobal.
This ship was the *Dunraven*, another fascinating ship which I was anxious to know more about. While our investigations continued, I kept constantly in contact with Renzo, through an Italian radio

ham, and found out that the *Jerusalem Post* had published an article on this wreck in 1979. I wrote to this Israeli newspaper and got them to send me the article; in it I read that unusually shaped bottles of soda water, very much like our own, had been found on the *Dunraven* too, which was therefore following the same route to the same destination.

The *Dunraven* had been built in Newcastle in 1873 and had sunk in 1876, but its design was more modern than that of our ship, and so it had probably been built few years later. The list of possible names was shrinking as more and more pieces of information came to light, but it was still too long. A further step forward was made when we heard some divers had found a human bone - identified as a left humerus - in the wreck. This meant lives had been lost when the ship capsized, and other names were crossed off the list. At this point there were only three names left. Renzo continued his meticulous search of the wreck in the hope of finding more clues, and eventually he did... The name started with the letter "C". It was all we needed: when Renzo gave me this piece of news over the phone, I shouted ecstatically down the line to him: "*Carnatic* It's the only ship still in the list that starts with a *C*"!

The history of the *Carnatic*

The Carnatic was a splendid steam-sail ship of the Peninsular & Oriental Steam Navigation Company, launched in the Samuda Brothers shipyards on December 8, 1862 and entered in the Register of Shipping on March 2 of the following year. With a length of 89 metres, width of 9 and draft of 5.3, it had an overall tonnage of 1,776 tons. The engine, built by Humphrys & Tennat in Deptford, produced 1,870 horsepower, fired by a steam boiler, and gave the ship a speed of 12 knots. During engine trials on April 18, 1863, it attained a top speed of 13.9 knots: no mean achievement and, although below the top speeds achievable under sail, definitely advantageous in the event of wind

dropping or when ascending the Red Sea with a headwind. Because these ships were able to ensure a steady speed and regular service, they were immediately used on the routes to India where precise arrivals and departures - unaffected by weather conditions - were essential for transporting mail, cargo and passengers.

The *Carnatic* made her maiden voyage on April 27, 1863, from Southampton to Alexandria. She soon entered service on the Suez-India route and right from her very first voyage round the Cape of Good Hope, proved to be fast and reliable, taking only 49 days from Southampton to Ceylon. Only a few weeks before the fatal voyage,

E

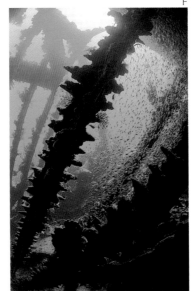

F

E - Protecting the foredeck was an awning held up by a row of metal poles - still clearly visible - fitted along both its sides.
Photograph by Roberto Rinaldi

F - Shipworms and salt water have eroded the ship's timbers and turned the vessel into an incongruous iron skeleton, populated by picturesque shoals of constantly moving fish.
Photograph by Vincenzo Paolillo

G - A diver explores the starboard bulwarks, in the stern section, where the lifeboat davits are still standing.
Photograph by Kurt Amsler

G

A

B

A - The ship's interior is an ideal shelter for dense shoals of glassfish, always a spectacular sight when encountered in the semi-darkness
Photograph by Roberto Rinaldi

B   Access to the interior of the vessel presents no major problems but attention must be paid not to stir up the thick sediment.
Photograph by Kurt Amsler

C - Glassfish usually gather in dense shoals and seek shelter close to coral reefs, but wrecks offer them even greater protection and provide an ideal habitat for this gregarious little sea-dwellers.
Photograph by Kurt Amsler

the *Carnatic* was involved in another incident: she ran aground on a sandbank off Alexandria, but luckily managed to float off with the high tide. She started out on her last voyage, from Suez bound for Bombay, on the evening of September 12, 1869, just about two months before the opening of the Suez Canal. The cargo had arrived from Liverpool on the steamship Venetian and was loaded onto the Carnatic at Suez. She left the port around 10 p.m. on a fine Sunday in September, with 230 people on board including both passengers and crew (though other sources say the number was far smaller). There were apparently 22 first-class passengers and 12 second-class, plus a servant and a child. Some of them were P & O employees, others were government officials sent out to supervise the laying of a telegraph cable, 525 miles long, in the Persian Gulf. The sea was calm, there was a light northerly wind and the ship made steady progress until 1.15 a.m. when the captain, P.B. Jones, was suddenly woken by shouts: "Breakers at the bow, Captain". "Helm to the left! Full speed astern!" But the ship's long, narrow hull had a very marked heading: although it cut through the waves with great ease, it took a long time to change direction. Three unbelievably long minutes passed, as the bow turned to the left with unnerving slowness: it just managed to miss the main reef of

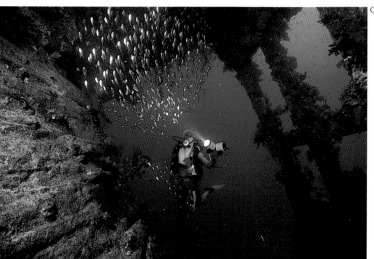

C

Sha'ab Abu Nuhâs, but not a small reef which was just one metre below the surface of the water. There was a great crash and a sound of breaking coral, and two-thirds of the hull lurched onto the reef and remained there, stuck fast. Everyone on board remained calm. An inspection was made by torchlight and, as the damage did not appear too serious, it was decided to wait until dawn to try to refloat the ship. The holds were emptied of their cargo to lighten the bow, but every effort was in vain. Meanwhile the bilges began to take on water, partly due to the northerly wind which had started to blow, pushing the ship until it was wedged against the reef. It was known that the *Sumatra*, another ship of the same line, was soon to

pass this same way and after spending the night on deck, waiting to be taken to the nearby island of Shadwan, the passengers expected the captain to give the order to lower the lifeboats. But he did not do so and life on board continued "as usual", with meals served at the usual times. By evening tension and concern among the passengers were growing and a delegation was sent to speak with the captain. But this delegation included the only two passengers who wanted to remain on board, having accepted the captain's argument about the ship being safe. So - like it or not - another night was spent on board, waiting for the rescue ship. During that night of September 14, however, at around 2 a.m., water came pouring into the engine room, extinguishing the boiler, and Captain Jones realized the ship was lost. The sea was getting rougher and water entering through numerous holes had completely filled the hull. At 10.50 a.m. when the three women passengers and the child had been transferred to the lifeboats, disaster struck: weighed down by the water it had taken on and weakened by the incessant pounding of the waves, the hull broke in two, or at least the stern section, no longer supported by the now-shattered reef, slipped from this precarious "mooring" and sank, taking with it twenty-seven passengers and crew members

D

E

F

G

(fifteen of them Europeans). The survivors climbed onto the bow, which was still above water, and in the three remaining lifeboats (out of seven) were ferried to the island of Shadwan. There cotton bales taken from the cargo were set alight and the only signal rocket salvaged was set off; it was seen by the *Sumatra* which during the evening - at 9 p.m. - had finally come into view. At 10 a.m. the following morning the passengers went aboard the rescue ship, which headed back towards Suez. Lloyd's very quickly organized an expedition to salvage the ship, led by Captain Henry D. Grant. This expedition was one of the first times ever that use was made of a deepsea diver. In actual fact, when the salvage ship reached Suez,

Captain Grant and his crew were told that the Carnatic had now completely sunk and was lying at a depth of 75 metres. They preferred to go and see for themselves and in fact discovered the bowsprit was still only just below the surface and numerous local divers, brought to the scene in small craft, were busy removing as much as the cargo they could reach. Stephen Saffery, the English diver, descended to the ship where he found two bodies; the head of one was wedged in a porthole, in an evident desperate attempt to escape drowning. Saffery succeeded in reaching the mail office, broke his way through the locked door and, within a few days, recovered 32,000 gold sovereigns of the 40,000 reportedly held in the safebox. The local divers

D - These large windows in the after part of the ship ensured there was plenty of light in the first-class saloon. On its last, tragic journey the Carnatic hosted 230 people among passengers and crew.
Photograph by Andrea Ghisotti

E, F, G - At the bottom of the holds there are still a few of the many bottles of wine and soda water that were part of the cargo, together with odd tools and pieces of equipment and machinery; the idea of taking home "curios" of the kind may be tempting but divers must not forget that the Carnatic and all it contains are now part of our heritage and as such must be left intact.
Photograph by Kurt Amsler

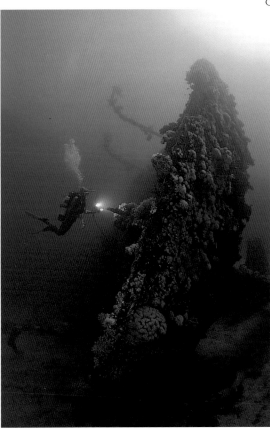

subsequently used to recover the ship's cargo demonstrated amazing diving skills and strength: with a rope tied around their waist they plunged to a depth of about 20 metres, got hold of one of the copper ingots that made up the cargo - each weighing between 20 and 35 kilos - and were then pulled back to the surface, after spending as long as 90 seconds underwater. 700 copper ingots and most of the mail bags were recovered in this way, but all trace of the other 8,000 sovereigns was lost. Could they still be somewhere among the twisted metal structures? The native divers continued to search after the salvage party had left, carrying away whatever they could find, until March 1870 when a stormy sea sent the bow section down to join the stern on the seafloor, and the wreck was consigned to oblivion for over a century.

Diving to the wreck

The dive to the *Carnatic* is not difficult since the ship rests on a sandy bed about 25 metres below the surface. The stern faces seaward and should be explored first. The vertical descent onto the wreck is a really thrilling experience since it makes you immediately aware of the structure of the vessel, with its strange low stern where you can see the large openings which were the windows of the first-class saloon. On the two flanks the lifeboat davits are still in place, and a marvellous mushroom coral formation adorns the one on the left side. The screw propeller has three blades; two of them point upwards and are covered with profusely growing soft corals. The huge rudder is also intact. The whole stern section can be easily explored from the interior: the planking has gone from the decks leaving only the metal supports, which makes it easy to move around the two decks. The first-class saloon was on the top deck, and the first-class cabins on the one below. This area is fairly dark and densely populated: swarms of glass-fish, turkeyfish, scorpionfish and crocodilefish have made their

A - At the end of the bow is a huge metal ring into which the bowsprit once fitted; fixed below it was the figure-head, in all likelihood removed during the Lloyd's recovery expedition, immediately after the shipwreck. Photograph by Kurt Amsler

B - The dive to the Carnatic presents no real problems - its depth is not excessive and there are no strong currents; explorers of this wreck of immense historic interest can therefore enjoy to the full the countless exciting discoveries that await them. Photograph by Kurt Amsler

C - Much of the stern of the ship has been colonized by hard corals: some large brain corals are among the most eye-catching. Photograph by Kurt Amsler

D - Though now extensively covered with concretions, parts of the machinery can still be spotted in the midships section, the most seriously damaged area of the vessel.
Photograph by
Kurt Amsler

E - A few bottles of wine lie amid the detritus on the bottom, strange relics of a shipwreck that has long ceased to hold dramatic memories.
Photograph by
Massimo Bicciato

D

E

home here. On leaving the stern move away from the hull, following the two masts which, pointing away from the reef, rest on the seafloor. The rigging is clad in stony coral and you can still see its shape perfectly. With a spot of luck you may run into a huge grouper which hangs around these parts. The midships section is little more than a tangle of metalwork - not surprisingly, since this is the part of the ship which gave way on the morning of September 14, 1869. But you can make out the engine area, the huge boiler further forward and the funnel, still in a reasonably well conserved state. The bow section, like the stern, is intact and here too, with the deck planking gone, there is easy access to the hold. Part of the cargo - the wooden boxes containing the bottles - was stored in the areas right on top of the bilges; the deck above was occupied by the crew's quarters. A fair portion of the dive should be spent visiting the bow for you will rarely have an opportunity to see another like it underwater. It closely resembles that of the sunken *Rhône* in the British Virgin Islands, long and slim like the bows of a clipper. The long bowsprit has unfortunately gone (only the ring which secured it remains), as has the figure-head once fixed below it: this was certainly recovered at the time of the Lloyd's expedition. On the flanks of the bow you can still clearly see the metal poles - now completely covered with concretions - which once supported an awning which covered the foredeck. Before leaving the *Carnatic*, a recommendation which is really more of a plea: this wreck is a historic monument of priceless value and it remained "intact" until 1987, when I visited the wreck for the first time. On that dive I came across splendid wooden blocks, fixtures and fittings, even a dainty sunshade which must have belonged to a 19th century lady passenger, and much more besides. I left everything exactly as I found it, so that future scuba divers might experience the same thrills we had, but I know the wreck has been extensively plundered by trophy-hunters. I appeal to future divers to touch nothing. This wonderful wreck belongs to all of us, let us conserve it!

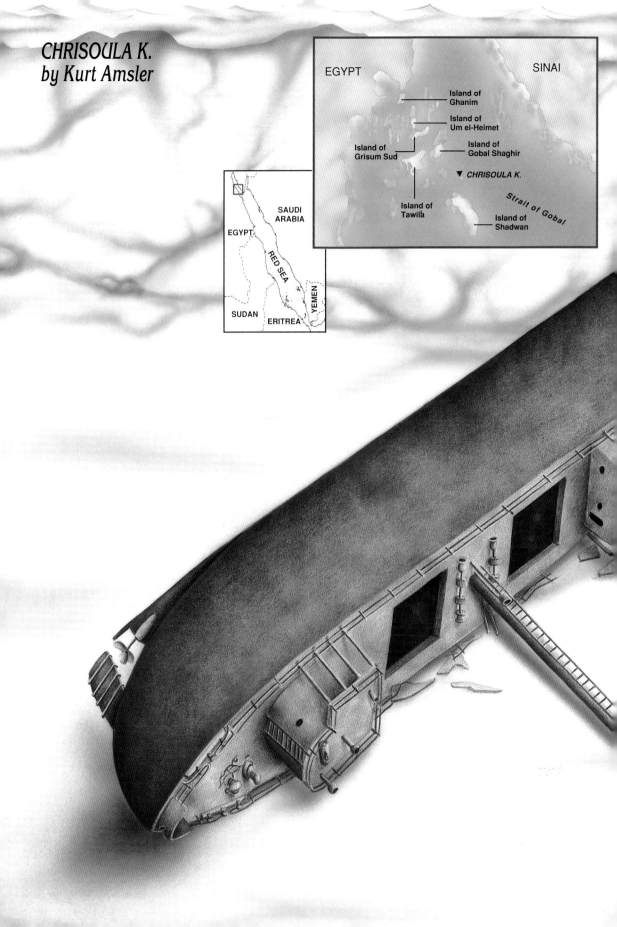

CHRISOULA K.
by Kurt Amsler

EGYPT   SINAI

Island of Ghanim

Island of Um el-Heimet

Island of Grisum Sud

Island of Gobal Shaghir

▼ CHRISOULA K.

Strait of Gobal

Island of Tawila

Island of Shadwan

SAUDI ARABIA

EGYPT

RED SEA

YEMEN

SUDAN

ERITREA

N ←

18 m

25 m

RATINGS

Finding site: easy.
Visibility: good to excellent.
Current: weak to strong.
Dive difficulty: easy.
Presence of lines or nets: none.
Historical interest: low.
Photographic interest: medium.
Biological interest: medium.

DATA FILE

Type of wreck: cargo ship.
Nationality: Greek.
Year of construction: 1954.
Tonnage: 3,700 tons.
Date of sinking: September 1981.
Cause of sinking: collision with reef.
Site position: close to Sha'ab Abu
        Nuhâs reef.
Geographical coordinates:
27°34'47.1"N, 33°55'37.9"W.
Distance from shore: against
        the reef.
Minimum depth: 18 metres.
Maximum depth: 25 metres.

THE CARGO BOAT
CHRISOULA K.

It was in September 1981 - the exact date is now not known - that the cargo boat *Chrisoula K.* ran into the Sha'ab Abu Nuhâs reef, the hazardous coral bank in the Red Sea along the shipping route to Gobal. Flying the Greek flag under the command of a Greek captain, Theodoros Kanellis, the vessel had come from Italy and was bound for Jeddah, in Saudi Arabia. Its cargo consisted essentially of blocks of stone. The reasons for the disaster are hard to understand: there is no obvious explanation why, as the ship steamed ahead with its engines at full throttle, it should have collided with the eastern side of the reef; whatever the possible cause, it was certainly not bad weather conditions or engine failure. The most likely reason is a navigation error, of much the same sort as has brought many other ships to a sad end at some point along the Sha'ab Abu Nuhâs reef. The violence of the impact threw the *Chrisoula K.* right onto the reef: the bow section broke away and was left perched on the coral bank; the remaining three-quarters of the vessel tipped over, falling onto the starboard flank with the stern pointing north-east. Fortunately the entire crew was rescued. During one of the first dives to the wreck, on October 29, 1981, we found a box containing assorted items that helped give a name to the then still unidentified wreck. This "treasure-trove" consisted of Captain Theodoros Kanellis's papers, numerous receipts (the last dated August 18, 1981), an Athens-Rome-Brindisi air ticket dated August 10, 1981 with the passenger name "Mr. Kanellis", a list of vaccinations, some telegrams, bills and business cards; there was also some correspondence exchanged with Clarion Marine & Co. From all this documentation - obtained during the dive made in October 1981 - it was possible to establish that the ship had gone down the previous month, September. And the name of the captain was no longer a mystery either.

A, B - In these two old photographs, the broken-off bow of the Chrisoula K. *is still lying on the coral reef of Sha'ab Abu Nuhâs; although the Greek cargo ship went down only in 1981, rough seas and the corrosive action of the salt water have totally destroyed this section of the vessel, now disappeared without trace.*
Photographs by Andrea Ghisotti

C - The stern is resting at the foot of the reef, on its starboard side. Its excellent state of conservation makes this section worth careful exploration.
Photograph by Alberto Muro

D - A diver explores the stern section of the wreck; clearly visible on the deck is the anchor capstan with its vertical windlass. Rising high behind it are the structures of the bridge deck.
Photograph by Vincenzo Paolillo

Diving to the wreck

Searching for the bow section of the *Chrisoula K.* is now a pointless exercise: rough seas and strong tides have long since swept it off the reef and obliterated every trace. Not even the smallest remains of this part of the ship are to be found underwater either. But the biggest and most interesting section of the *Chrisoula K.* still lies at the foot of the reef, resting on its starboard flank; it forms practically a right-angle with the coral wall, the stern facing north-north-east. When still at a certain distance, divers approaching the wreck can tell the ship was carrying blocks of stone since much of the cargo is strewn all around it.
Before your dive take the direction and speed of currents into consideration, although at Sha'ab Abu Nuhâs they are rarely rapid and usually south-flowing.
Your cover boat should drop anchor close to the reef, so the visit to the wreck can be started from the stern; it is definitely best to start here, at a depth of 25 metres, and then to work your way up along the portside bulwarks. When you reach the deepest point of the site, start your exploration of the *Chrisoula K.* by taking a look at the screw and rudder: the unusual grooves running their length are an interesting feature. Continue along the hull until you reach the bulwarks; at this point it is already obvious that the vessel has no proper deck since its superstructures start just a few metres from the place where the ship broke in two. In this area there are doors facing sternwards, through which you can peer into the ship's interior.
Finning your way along the bulwarks you come to the aft hold; the huge main mast is here too, bent horizontal and pointing towards the open sea.
The holds appear to be empty as all the cargo left on board is now in great piles at the bottom, on the starboard side. It is evident from this exploration of the *Chrisoula K.* that the ship must have had a clean-cut line: right up to the

D

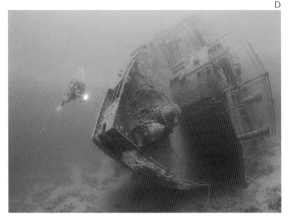

E

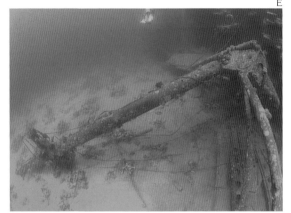

F

G

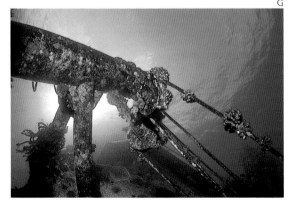

E - Sloping towards starboard in the direction of the open sea, the tall main mast is now almost horizontal with the seabed. As this photograph shows, some of the pulleys used to move the cargo booms are still attached to the crosstrees.
Photograph by Vincenzo Paolillo

F - The huge four-bladed central screw is at a depth of 25 metres; like the rudder, it suffered little damage when it hit the sandy bottom.
Photograph by Kurt Amsler

G - Massive coral formations have colonized the pulley tackle of this derrick.
Photograph by Kurt Amsler

superstructures and bridge there were no welds in the bulwarks. The bridge is easily accessible since there are numerous ways in. If you intend to venture into other areas inside the ship (galley, washrooms, cabins, engine room and many other parts can be explored without problems), make sure you are equipped with a powerful torch. Also remember one of the fundamental rules for safe dives to wreck sites: never lose sight of the light that comes in through openings, for it is the essential pointer to your way out! Once your tour of the interior is complete, fin along above the wreck once again: you are bound to notice the severe damage suffered by parts of the

A

B

C

D

E

A - The remains of the **Chrisoula K.** are lying on the starboard flank, as is evident from this rather unusual view of the wreck; the structures visible in the background are those of the bridge deck.
Photograph by Alberto Muro

B - Two twobar anemonefish fin their way around the deck; the wreck of the **Chrisoula K.** has become a perfect habitat for many marine species, who now reside here in great numbers.
Photograph by Alberto Muro

C - Scores and scores of glassfish swimming among the twisted girders move all together to the rhythm of the currents.
Photograph by Vincenzo Paolillo

D - Lying on the seabed like a felled giant is the main mast together with the large crosstrees that supported its weight.
Photograph by Vincenzo Paolillo

E - This diver appears to be "scaling" the vertical wall of the bridge deck; with no problems caused by currents this is a thoroughly enjoyable dive, thanks also to the delightfully limpid water.
Photograph by Kurt Amsler

superstructures; a pile of twisted girders can also be spotted on the seabed. Your exploration of all the most exciting parts of the *Chrisoula K.* is now over.

Also worth examining is the foremast, lying on the reef; the forward hold was practically destroyed by the tremendous impact of the collision.

The dive to the Greek cargo boat is fairly simple, with no particular hazards: the current at this spot is not strong and the sea is generally calm.

In the fifteen years that have passed since the *Chrisoula K.* sank, the ship has gradually turned into an artificial reef: dense schools of fish hover in the water over the superstructures,

F

G

H

I

J

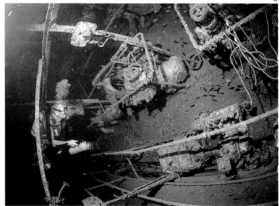

while thousands of glassfish now resident in the interiors glint in the rays of the sun, creating a truly spectacular scenario.

The wreck also offers an interesting site for biological fieldwork, since measurements can be taken to monitor the annual speed of growth of the soft and hard corals now present in huge colonies.

F - With their thick coat of enamel, bathtubs stand up longer to the salt water's corrosive action.
Photograph by Kurt Amsler

G - Pressure gauges, control boards, gate-valves: the equipment in the engine room can still be identified down to the very smallest detail.
Photograph by Vincenzo Paolillo

H - Exploring the interior of the vessel is a truly exciting experience but, as always in these cases, it is essential for divers not to stir up sediment and never to lose sight of light sources, and then risk remaining trapped in the wreck.
Photograph by Kurt Amsler

I, J - Powerful torches are needed to properly explore the interior of the wreck, where there are a great many structural and technical features of interest.
Photographs by Kurt Amsler

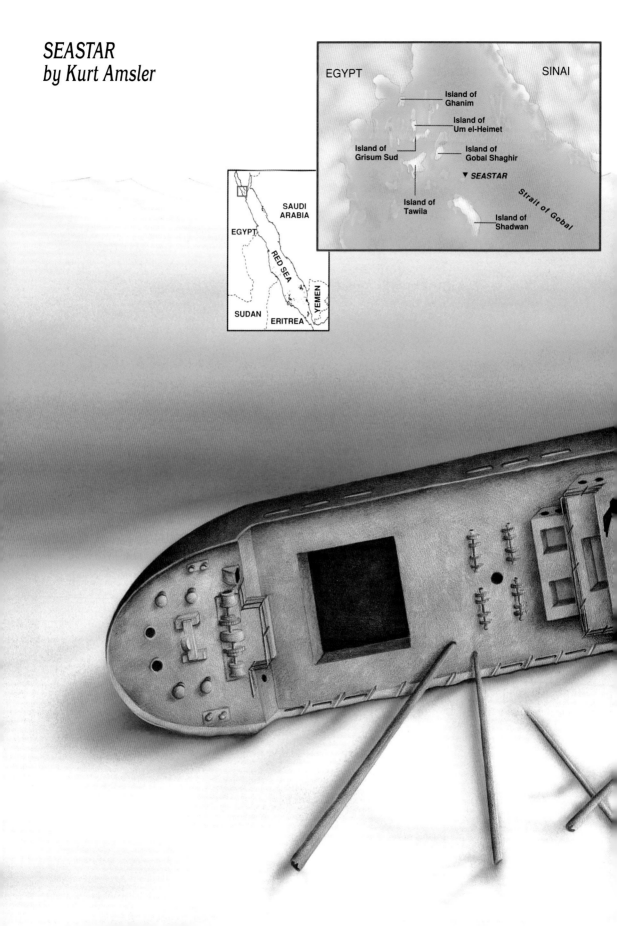

SEASTAR
by Kurt Amsler

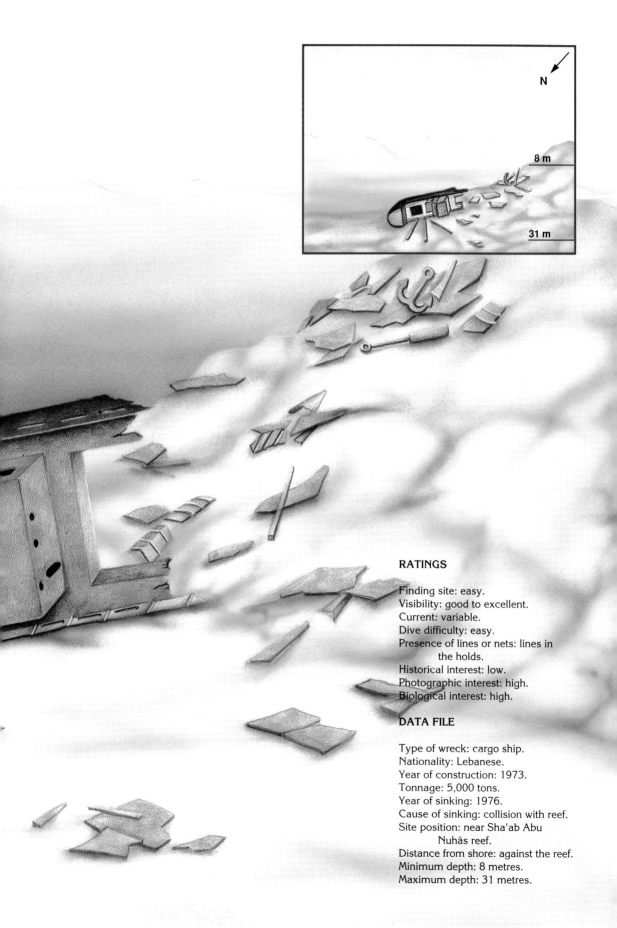

RATINGS

Finding site: easy.
Visibility: good to excellent.
Current: variable.
Dive difficulty: easy.
Presence of lines or nets: lines in
        the holds.
Historical interest: low.
Photographic interest: high.
Biological interest: high.

DATA FILE

Type of wreck: cargo ship.
Nationality: Lebanese.
Year of construction: 1973.
Tonnage: 5,000 tons.
Year of sinking: 1976.
Cause of sinking: collision with reef.
Site position: near Sha'ab Abu
        Nuhâs reef.
Distance from shore: against the reef.
Minimum depth: 8 metres.
Maximum depth: 31 metres.

THE CARGO BOAT *SEASTAR*

Little is known about the *Seastar* and its history or about the reasons for its fatal collision with the Sha'ab Abu Nuhâs reef. The only certain fact concerns the cargo it was carrying at the time of the disaster: several tons of lentils, still to be seen in rows of now open sacks in the hold; "stored" in the depths of the sea, they provide food for the myriads of fish that have made the wrecked cargo ship their home. The vessel, which flew the Lebanese flag, had a tonnage of 5,000 tons and was about 60 metres long. The last time the name of the *Seastar* was entered in shipping records was in 1976, at Port Suez; under the command of Captain Tassos Adrianopulos, the ship left its anchorage in the early morning and made for the open sea. How the cargo boat came to hit the Sha'ab Abu Nuhâs reef remains a mystery although many other vessels - before and after it - have shared the same fate. A fairly likely hypothesis is that, on account of the war being waged in the area at that time, seamarks essential to ships plying these waters had been removed; this made the voyage through the channel leading to Gobal a practically impossible venture, like passing through the eye of a needle. Even today, it would be unthinkable for a ship to sail safely through the Strait without modern navigational instruments and, at night, the aid of beacons. Although we have no way of knowing the exact reasons why the *Seastar* collided with the coral bank, it is certain the ship was travelling at speed and hit the sharp eastern edge of the reef. Observing the position of the wreck it is evident that, had its course been set just a few metres wider - and had fate been kinder - it would have cleared the reef and avoided the collision. For eight years after the disaster, the bows section of the *Seastar* remained on the reef above water level, a sombre warning to passing ships.

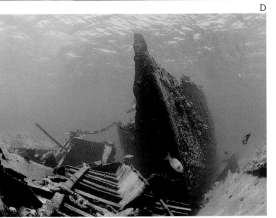

A - The Sha'ab Abu Nuhâs reef is best described as a ships' graveyard, scattered with so many wrecks as to suspect the place is cursed: pictured in this archive photo are the remains of the *Seastar, left, the* grounded freighter San Juan, centre, and the stem of an unidentified cargo boat, right.
Photograph by Kurt Amsler

B - Still visible above the reef when this photo was taken in 1982, the stem of the *Seastar was* swallowed up by the sea in 1984; this section of the vessel has since been completely broken up by the waves.
Photograph by Kurt Amsler

C - The stern lies at a depth of 31 metres, at the foot of the coral cliff that surrounds the reef; the position of the wreck, exposed to very strong currents, makes the dive impossible when the sea is rough.
Photograph by Roberto Rinaldi

D - The part of the ship from stem to forward hold is now a huge, shapeless mass of twisted plates of metal, providing welcome shelter to myriads of fish.
Photograph by Roberto Rinaldi

E

F

E - In one of the holds, a diver illuminates a dense shoal of tiny silver fish. Photograph by Kurt Amsler

G - A diver examines the top part of what must have been the pylon supporting the radio antenna. Photograph by Kurt Amsler

F - Pictured here beneath the massive bulk of the stern are the huge rudder and four-blade central propeller screw. Photograph by Roberto Rinaldi

H - Still standing on deck is one of the masts, its wind-braces - like the machines in the foreground - now encrusted with corals. Photograph by Roberto Rinaldi

G

H

Diving to the wreck

Continuously rocked by waves and occasionally battered by storms, the bows of the ship eventually disappeared beneath the surface for good. But on top of the reef and down its sloping side are still numerous pieces of twisted metal, the mast, some loading platforms and an enormous anchor.

The after section of the Lebanese cargo ship, more than 50 metres long, is instead lying at the foot of the cliff, on its starboard side. Exploration of the wreck, now not in a very good state of conservation, takes divers to normally acceptable depths: the pieces still on the reef and the huge anchor are at between 8 and 15 metres, the highest point of the portside bulwarks is at 16 metres, the stern is at 31 metres.

The *Seastar* lies by the east corner of the reef; if the sea is at all rough, the dive should not be attempted and would in any case be practically impossible.

The wreck of the *Seastar* is not far from that of the *Chrisoula K.*: a diver who is physically fit and has an adequate supply of air can swim along the reef, sheltered from currents, and explore both, starting from the *Chrisoula K.*, which is further away from the reef.

The *Seastar* broke in two across its forward hold; great shoals of young fish now hover inside the massive hull. Much of the cargo, mainly sacks of lentils, is enveloped and even totally covered in concretions of algae.

For years the lentils have served as food for thousands of fish: it's hard to say whether they are still edible but countless parrotfish, triggerfish and other fish in dense shoals can be seen continuously making their way in and out of the hull. Make sure you are equipped with a powerful torch so you miss nothing of this amazing explosion of marine life inside the wreck. The midship section is entirely occupied by the superstructures and main deck, now colonized to an amazing extent by corals, alcyonarians especially. They grow in particular abundance along the

A

B

metal cables, on the bulwarks and rails and in the darker parts of the hull. Behind the superstructures is the huge aft hold.

Other easily recognizable parts of the ship - like the mast and loading platforms - are instead no longer in position since they collapsed onto the deck and slipped down to the bottom. There is a fairly spacious poop deck with a large winch still visible at its centre.

Your exploration of the wreck is now practically over. Make your way to the starboard flank, at a depth of 31 metres, and then return towards the bows, first passing beneath the huge propeller.

From this point follow the portside bulwarks as far as the reef, bringing your dive to an end in fairly shallow water.

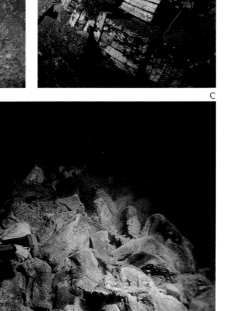

C

D

A - Large schools of fish swim about in the holds and between the superstructures on deck rich in stony coral formations: prominent amongst them is the ubiquitous, reddish-orange anthias.
Photograph by Roberto Rinaldi

B - Piled up in the holds are numerous wooden crates, their contents long since removed.
Photograph by Roberto Rinaldi

C - A diver examines the sacks of lentils that formed the cargo of the Seastar.
Photograph by Kurt Amsler

D - Access to the huge holds is easy for divers wishing to explore, but powerful torches are a must; it is also advisable to move with caution.
Photograph by Roberto Rinaldi

E

F

I

G

J

H

H - Immortalized in this photo is a magnificent sohal surgeonfish, no stranger to the wreck of the Seastar. *Photograph by Roberto Rinaldi*

I - The growth of soft corals seems more luxuriant along the metal cables and rails, perhaps because the nutrients on which they depend are more abundant here. Photograph by Kurt Amsler

J - One of the Seastar's *anchors lies on the reef just a few metres below the surface, indicating the position of the stem before it was broken up by the force of the waves. Photograph by Kurt Amsler*

E, F - Although torn from its housing, the main mast is practically still in one piece and is now lying flat on the seabed. Photographs by Kurt Amsler

G - On the deck especially the alcyonarians have now grown to an amazing size. Photograph by Roberto Rinaldi

SALEM EXPRESS
by Kurt Amsler

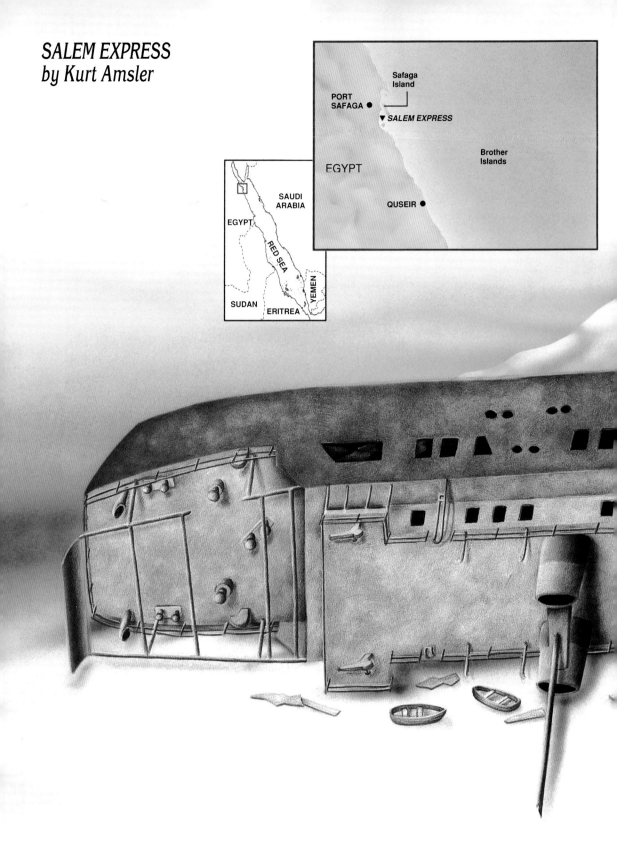

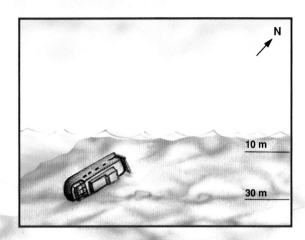

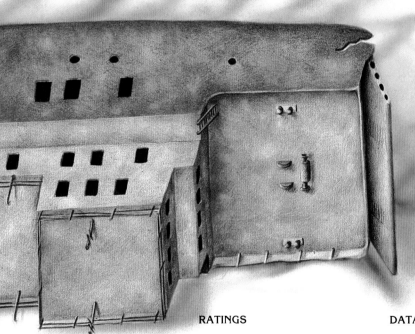

RATINGS

Finding site: easy.
Visibility: good to excellent
Current: weak
Dive difficulty: easy
Presence of lines or nets: a few
Historical interest: low
Photographic interest: high
Biological interest: medium

DATA FILE

Type of wreck: ferry.
Nationality: Egyptian.
Year of construction: 1966.
Tonnage: 1,105 tons (gross).
Date of sinking: 16/12/1991
Cause of sinking: collision with reef.
Site position: a short way south of
        Hyndman Reef, opposite
        Port Safaga.
Geographical coordinates:
        26°38'24.5"N, 34°03'40.2"W.
Distance from shore: against
        the reef.
Minimum depth: 10 metres.
Maximum depth: 30 metres.

THE FERRY *SALEM EXPRESS*

Only a tragic, fatal human error could have caused the sinking of the *Salem Express*. The ferry had left Jeddah, in Saudi Arabia, bound for Port Safaga in Egypt. Most of the passengers on board were pilgrims on their way home from Mecca.

Close to midnight on December 15, 1991, the ship was making headway through fairly rough seas along a channel of deep water between the mainland and Hyndman Reef, on its charted course. It was only 11 kilometres from its destination when disaster struck. South of Hyndman Reef three huge banks of coral just break the surface; the engines of the *Salem Express* were running at full throttle when it hit the one furthest west.

The effects of the collision were devastating: a rip more than 10 metres long left a gaping hole in the forward part of the hull and the violence of the impact made the huge stern door burst open. The ferry immediately started to take on enormous quantities of water through the two openings and in a matter of minutes the huge vessel - 100 metres long - was swallowed up by the sea.

Of the 690 passengers on board only 180 survived and the way in which the crew behaved as the ship was sinking was later fiercely criticized. Rescue operations were badly organized, inefficient and altogether chaotic: the lifeboats still firmly attached to the davits are chilling evidence of the speed with which the ferry went down, and the terrible drama of those moments. The *Salem Express* was a sizeable vessel with a gross tonnage of 1,105 tons, much like the heavyweights that still sail the seas of the Middle East, hefty but also angular.

To provide shelter from the burning sun, corrugated iron roofing had been fitted on the decks; to board the ferry, vehicles had to be driven through an upward-opening door at the head of the ship (a system now prohibited, for obvious safety reasons). The ferry had two engines (evident from its two funnels and two screw propellers), a fairly common feature of vessels of this type.

A - Still perfectly legible on the square stern is the name of this Egyptian ferry; 510 of its passengers perished when it sank in December 1991.

B - The wreck lies on its starboard flank, making it easy for divers to "fly" over its port side and examine its features from close quarters; in this picture we can see the promenade deck with its high rails, and some portholes of passenger cabins.

C - The lifeboats still attached to their davits are dramatic evidence of both the speed with which the vessel sank and the impossibility for the passengers to be rescued by the crew.

D - It is still possible to make out the supporting structure of a makeshift, corrugated metal roof installed on the main deck and poop deck to afford passengers shelter from the burning rays of the sun.

Diving to the wreck

The wreck is lying on its starboard side at the foot of the reef, its prow pointing north-north-west, its stern south-south-east; the deepest part is 30 metres down, while the portside is 10 metres from the surface.
Its size makes the wreck of the *Salem Express* an awe-inspiring sight and yet, since it is not situated at a great depth, divers can fin their way right around it and explore the deck and superstructures thoroughly.
Some years have now passed since the ship met its tragic fate but at their first glimpse of the wreck divers are bound to be profoundly moved.
And it goes without saying that any visitor to the wreck must show the deepest respect for the hundreds of people who perished so tragically.
The dive starts from the stern which, thanks to its massive square shape, can be made out even at some distance.
The size of the port side propeller makes it an awesome object; it is still fairly "clean", having yet to be colonized by benthic organisms, unlike the starboard one.
This is instead to be found under the hull, away from the light, and the soft red corals that have "taken up residence" on its surfaces (hub and blades in particular) have already grown to an impressive size.
The dive along the hull is not particularly exciting and offers nothing of special interest.
It is best to fin your way over the rail on the port side of the vessel and to head for the still well-preserved main deck and poop deck. Morning is the time when light conditions are at their best; in the afternoon this part of the *Salem Express* is in shadow.
As you come to the stern you see a metal structure, what is left of the deck "roofing"; in this section of the ship the bollards and mooring cables, airducts and a winch are still clearly visible.
After reaching the first superstructures continue for about 15 metres on the poop deck, where you will see the two davits. Fin your way along the bulwarks on the starboard side, down to deeper water; you will eventually find yourself looking at the lifeboats, now resting on the seabed but still roped to the ship. Numerous pieces of the sheet-metal roofing have broken away and lie scattered on the bottom. From a distance you can also make out the two enormous funnels, each with a huge letter "S" set in a laurel wreath on either side; a catwalk connects the two. From this point it is about 20 metres to the upper deck, straight up above the main deck.
On the roof you can see the antennas, still in place, and a large radar device facing - now pointlessly - towards the open sea. The dive to the *Salem Express* is a unique and moving experience, of the kind scuba divers who visit wrecks have to get accustomed to.
Through the windows of the bridge you can peer into the ferry's interior.

The total emptiness that greets your curious gaze may come as a surprise: all the objects not fixed in place at the time of the collision have fallen down to the bottom corners on the starboard side, where they now lie in great piles. At this point of the dive you will be facing the foredeck and the main door; if you continue to explore along the portside bulwarks you eventually come to the stempost, which suffered serious damage. Nearby is a huge anchor hanging from the hawsehole.
When preparing your ascent, your best route is to fin along the portside rail where the water is about 10 metres deep: your remaining supply of air should be more than enough to let you surface unhurriedly.

E

F

E - Set in a laurel wreath on the enormous portside funnel is a huge "S", the first letter of the ship's name.

F - The wreck is relatively young and its structures are still free of sediment and encrustations formed by marine organisms; although somewhat bare, the interior of the bridge, seen here, is in practically perfect condition.

All the photos of the dive to the Salem Express *were taken by Kurt Amsler.*

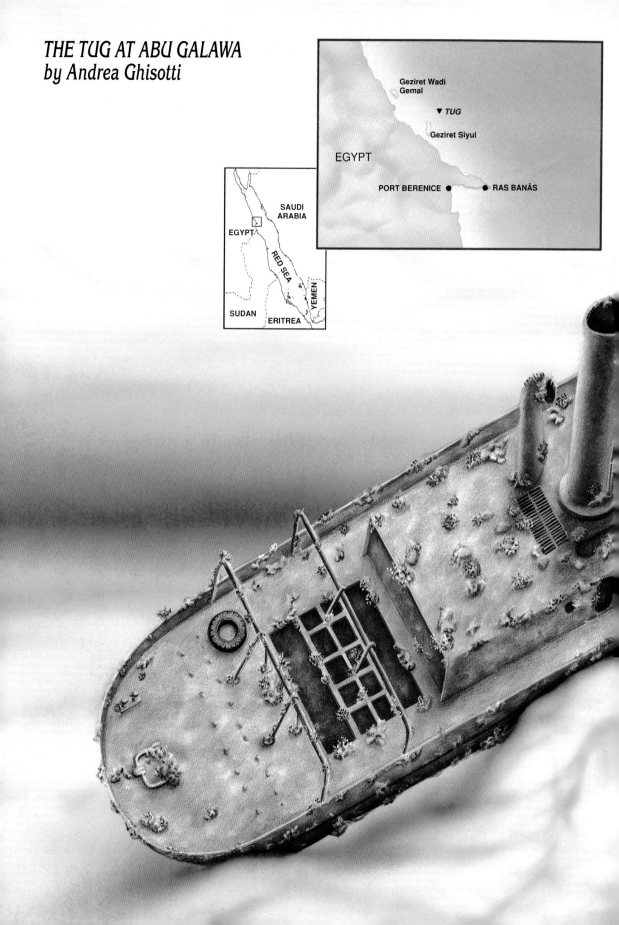

THE TUG AT ABU GALAWA
by Andrea Ghisotti

Geziret Wadi Gemal

▼ *TUG*

Geziret Siyul

EGYPT

PORT BERENICE ●————● **RAS BANÂS**

SAUDI ARABIA

EGYPT

RED SEA

YEMEN

SUDAN

ERITREA

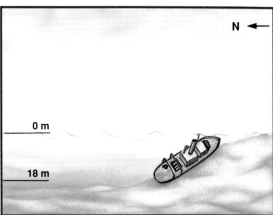

RATINGS

Finding site: medium difficulty.
Visibility: excellent.
Current: weak.
Dive difficulty: easy.
Presence of lines and nets: none.
Historical interest: low.
Photographic interest: high.
Biological interest: medium.

DATA FILE

Type of wreck: tug.
Nationality: possibly Egyptian.
Year of construction: unknown.
Tonnage: 300 tons (estimated).
Date of sinking: unknown.
Cause of sinking: collision with reef.
Site position: north side of Abu
    Galawa reef.
Distance from shore: against
    the reef.
Minimum depth: emerging from
    the surface.
Maximum depth: 18 metres.

THE TUG AT ABU GALAWA

What can a tug be doing here in the Red Sea, far away from ports, pontoons, dry docks and the many heavy tasks it was designed to carry out? Perhaps it was called out to rescue one of the endless ships that have gone aground on this reef, and then succumbed to tragedy itself?

It is difficult to say: the tug sank many years ago and the little importance of the wreck makes research very difficult.

All we can do is accept it as one of many obscure tragedies at sea, without trying to pinpoint the exact sequence of events, date and name. Careful observation of the wreck can provide a few clues and make the dive more fun.

First and foremost, the site: Abu Galawa, a small reef with plentiful flora and fauna not far from Ras Qulan, the departure point for all cruises in the area of Ras Banâs and Zabargad.

The wreck, situated on the north side of the reef, has much to tell visitors about the dramatic end of the tug. The bow is very close to the surface, almost emerging from the water, and a rip in its plating shows the point of collision with the reef.

All things considered, the damage is limited: no furious tempests, crumpled metal and vessel dashed to pieces by the force of the waves. But the leak clearly let in sufficient water to sink the tug which slid gently to the bottom, the stern at 18 metres, the rest of the vessel resting on the sloping wall of the reef.

A shipwreck of the kind can only happen in a dead calm sea - something rarely encountered around these parts but, ironically, more perilous than a slightly choppy one. With no breakers to create tell-tale foam, reefs just below the surface remain completely hidden.

And to sail a ship through an area thick with reefs not clearly indicated on nautical maps is like playing Russian roulette.

A - The wreck of the tug at Abu Galawa rests at an angle on the gently sloping reef. Its stern is at a depth of about 18 metres.
Photograph by Massimo Bicciato

B - Waves and currents tend to be forceful in such shallow water but the wreck is in an excellent state of conservation.
Photograph by Massimo Bicciato

C - Clearly visible midships is the tall funnel; its long, narrow shape makes it seem likely that the boat was built in the early post-war period.
Photograph by Andrea Ghisotti

D - The hull is sloping over onto its starboard flank, a position which allows divers at the stern to fin along under the keel to the point where they can spot the screw and rudder.
Photograph by Andrea Ghisotti

E - Still on board - and in an excellent state of conservation - are the huge truck tyres used as fenders, still a common practice today.
Photograph by Andrea Ghisotti

Diving to the wreck

The vessel is amazingly well conserved, considering it lies in such shallow water. The sea here is crystal-clear which means you can get a panoramic view of the whole wreck, an underwater spectacle not easily forgotten. To witness it to full advantage, move away from the reef, finning seaward on the north side; drop down a little when you are at a certain distance from the stern, and float midwater; from here you can admire the scene as though it were part of a film. The tug is gently resting on its starboard flank, and sloping just enough to let you see, on the left, the screw half-hidden in the sandy

F - The dive presents no particular difficulties and the crystal-clear water makes it possible to examine every minor detail of the wreck, heightening the enjoyment of a truly exhilarating dive.
Photograph by Andrea Ghisotti

G - Although erosion has destroyed part of the partition walls on the bridge deck, it is easy to locate the bathroom with its still recognizable sanitary fittings.
Photograph by Massimo Bicciato

H - Machinery in the engine room are still in a very good state of conservation; not being subject to the currents, it is covered by thick layers of sediment.
Photograph by Andrea Ghisotti

I - This porthole, with its window still intact, suggests that the tug went down in circumstances that were far from tragic; it also shows that only a limited amount of damage has been done by the sea.
Photograph by Massimo Bicciato

seafloor. On board there are still the huge truck tyres - highly resistant and almost indestructible - which tugs always use as fenders. Concretions and profusely growing stony coral cover the wreck, an indication that the tug did not sink recently. The shape of the vessel, with its tall, narrow funnel, suggests it was a tug of a certain age; judging by its rather elongated form, it probably dates back to the immediate post-war period, or perhaps even earlier. However, it has to be remembered that tugs have a long working life and the date of its sinking could be later. Visiting the vessel presents no particular difficulties, save the engine room which is dark and thick with sediment that could

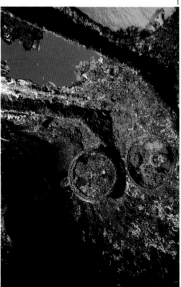

be stirred up by the slightest movement of your fins. Only the most experienced divers, who know how to move in limited space without creating suspended sediment, should venture into this area. Apart from the usual wall of silver glass-fish, you can admire - still in place - many of the ship's fixtures and fittings, mechanical features, lamps and containers. The bridge area with adjoining cabins and W.C. are easily accessed and have consequently - to a certain extent - been "cleaned out" by previous divers.
But there are still a few nice objects, including (I hope) an attractive, antiquated-looking fan which makes me date the tug to around World War Two.

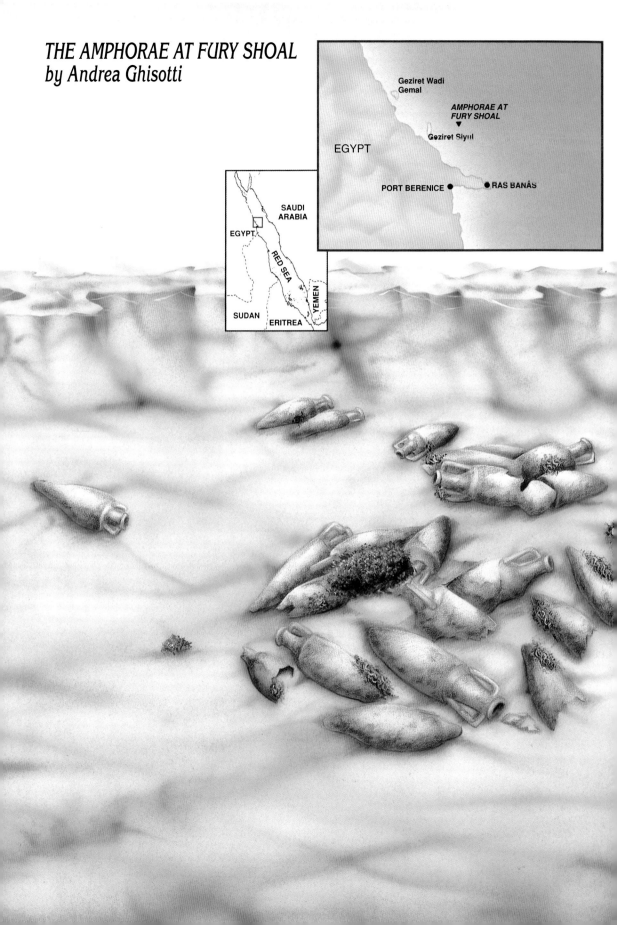

THE AMPHORAE AT FURY SHOAL
by Andrea Ghisotti

Geziret Wadi Gemal

AMPHORAE AT FURY SHOAL

EGYPT

Geziret Siyul

PORT BERENICE

RAS BANÂS

SAUDI ARABIA

EGYPT

RED SEA

SUDAN

ERITREA

YEMEN

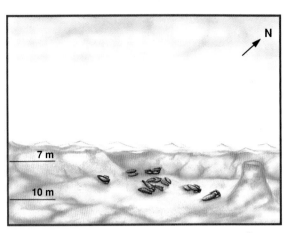

RATINGS

Finding site: easy.
Visibility: excellent.
Current: none.
Dive difficulty: easy.
Presence of lines and nets: none.
Historical interest: high.
Photographic interest: high.
Biological interest: low.

DATA FILE

Type of wreck: Roman cargo ship.
Year of construction: unknown.
Date of sinking: unknown.
Cause of sinking: probable collision
        with reef.
Geographical coordinates:
        24°09.32'N, 35°41.13'E.
Site position: Fury Shoal coral barrier.
Distance from shore: against
        the reef.
Minimum depth: 7 metres.
Maximum depth: 10 metres.

THE AMPHORAE AT FURY SHOAL

In ancient times the port of Berenice had strategic importance, not because it offered convenient facilities, good anchorage, fresh water supplies or good boatbuilding yards but because it was situated in one of the very few bays of any real use along the Egyptian side of the Red Sea and offered protection against the prevailing northerly winds that constantly swept that coast. Berenice was in fact a far-from-pleasant, insalubrious place of ill repute, an outpost abandoned for many months of the year. It had no source of fresh water, which had to be brought from Kalalat, five miles away. The atrocious amount of hard work caused by this fact alone - when a fleet of ships was about to set sail - is beyond belief... And yet Berenice became the main supplies base for all the Roman ships heading south to the African coast or to Eudaimon - present-day Aden - which was the biggest trading centre on the route to the East. In Rome there was great demand for oriental merchandise, spices in particular, and traders' mark-ups were incredibly high, even a hundred times the price originally paid. This very profitable business meant that an enormous number of ships plied these waters in the days of the Empire. It therefore follows that a good many cargo ships must have succumbed to the treacherous reefs, perilous currents and prevailing northerly winds and that their remains must be widely scattered on the floor of the whole Red Sea. And yet finds have been few and no thorough, official archaeological expeditions have been organized to gather information on ancient wrecks. Initiatives may have been discouraged by the fact that this part of the Red Sea is "off the beaten track" and under military control, so off limits to most people. However, the Bicciato brothers from Milan recently obtained a permit to operate charter boats around Ras Banâs, the promontory at the eastern end of the bay were Port Berenice is situated. In November

in the midst of the Red Sea they had lain undisturbed for twenty centuries. Later, when travelling in these parts, I went to visit the scene of this discovery and found it a truly fascinating place. It lies within a large system of coral ridges and hummocks called Fury Shoal, a series of reef formations with varying structural features. The wreck is sited in a small inlet where the night can be spent when there is a prevailing northerly wind blowing. The amphorae are lying on the sandy bottom at a depth of 7-10 metres, mainly grouped at the foot of the reef. They might have been thrown overboard to lighten a vessel in trouble or part of a cargo could have gone sliding into the water after collision with the reef;

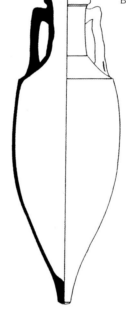

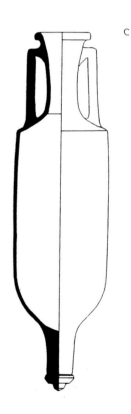

1991, during one of their first cruises, the remains of an ancient wreck were discovered by Pierfranco Dilenge, a well-known Italian photographer. Dilenge was to take part in a night dive and, while waiting for dark, he went for a brief swim with his mask and fins: he was astounded when, in shallow water, he suddenly noticed about thirty amphorae scattered on the sandy seabed below him. They were beautiful amphorae, long and slender in shape: in Mediterranean waters they would never have survived so long - divers motivated solely by greed and selfishness would have seen to that! - but here

A - The amphorae scattered on the seabed around Fury Shoal are all that remains of a Roman cargo boat, sunk some two thousand years ago.
Photograph by Andrea Ghisotti.

B, C - Illustrated here are the two kinds of amphorae found in these waters; from their shape they would seem to be wine amphorae, although it is difficult to explain their presence in the Red Sea.

D

Diving to the wreck

The dive to the amphorae is a thrilling journey back through time and, being the water so shallow, you might prefer to leave your breathing apparatus behind, but only with an air tank will you be able to indulge your curiosity without haste. Never more than here has the rule "look but do not touch" been applicable, so please let civilized behaviour prevail. In 1994 a group of divers tried to steal some of the amphorae, but were caught by the local police and punished. It is to be hoped their misguided and shameful course of action and its consequences will discourage other unscrupulous divers from similar acts of vandalism.

E

F

alternatively, to add a note of mystery and drama, the amphorae could have contained something precious, perhaps fine olivine from nearby Zabargad which had been stolen and then left here "for safekeeping", until it could be retrieved (which it never was). Anxious to solve the enigma, I used a knife to probe the sandy floor under and around the amphorae and, digging with my hands, came across the unmistakable timbers of an old vessel. So I had my evidence: a ship had sunk and its keel is still there, waiting to reveal all sorts of possible surprises if a proper archaeological exploration of the site were organized. The amphorae are long and slender with a double-curved shape: some of them are covered with concretions and stuck hard and fast to the seafloor, others are adorned with spectacular coral, unusual on finds more common to Mediterranean waters. There are assorted shapes but all of them typical of the wine amphorae used in Republican and Imperial times. The most numerous appear to be "amphorae of the Kos tradition". This Dodecanese island produced excellent wine which - as Cato relates in *De Agricultura* - was imitated in Italy by immersing grapes in sea-water, to obtain the characteristic flavour of wine from this Greek island. To make their product look even more genuine, the Italian swindlers cunningly also copied the amphorae, which

became distinctive wares labelled as "in the Greek or Kos tradition". But what was a boat loaded with wine - be it authentic or "imitation" - doing in the Red Sea? Perhaps this particular cargo was intended to get merchants drunk and obtain better trading prices, to grace the richly spread tables of the Empire or to make life in Berenice more bearable for some Roman official far from home? In ancient times, however, amphorae had a multitude of uses, besides holding wine and oil. There is no knowing what might be contained in the amphorae at Fury Shoal although as shape often denoted contents, in this case it is very probably wine.

D - Amphorae were the containers most used by the peoples of the ancient world, and the amphora was in fact one of the most common Roman units for measuring capacity, corresponding to approximately 25 cubic decimetres today.
Photograph by Andrea Ghisotti

E - Large Roman cargo vessels - called onerarie from the Latin word onus, meaning weight - could carry as many as two thousand amphorae, neatly stacked in wooden racks.
Photograph by Massimo Bicciato

F - The Roman ship had called - or was about to call - at the port of Berenice which, in ancient times, was a major supplies base and trading centre on the route to the East.
Photograph by Massimo Bicciato

THE CARGO BOAT AT ZABARGAD
by Massimo Bicciato

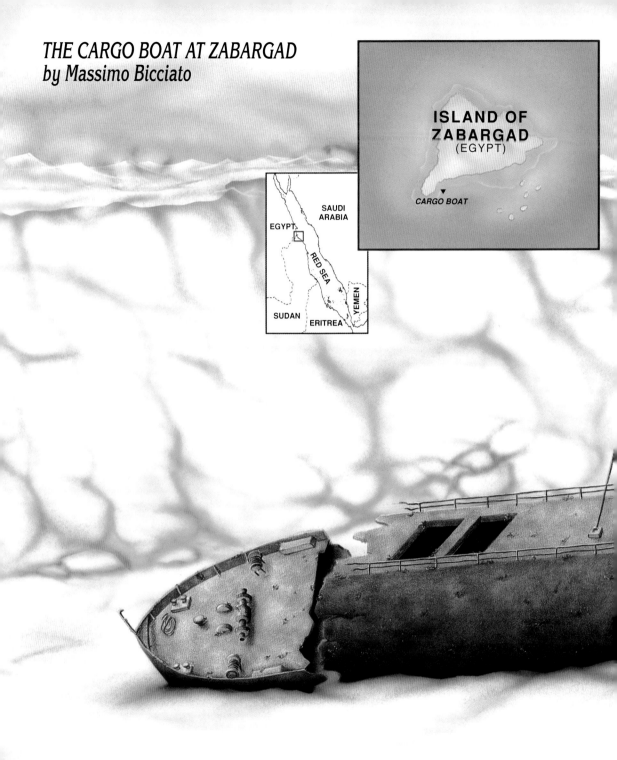

ISLAND OF
ZABARGAD
(EGYPT)

▼
CARGO BOAT

SAUDI
ARABIA

EGYPT

RED SEA

YEMEN

SUDAN   ERITREA

RATINGS

Finding site: easy.
Visibility: fairly good to excellent.
Current: weak to very strong.
Dive difficulty: easy to medium.
Presence of lines or nets: none.
Historical interest: low.
Photographic interest: high.
Biological interest: medium.

DATA FILE

Type of wreck: cargo ship.
Nationality: unknown.
Year of construction: unknown.
Tonnage: unknown.
Date of sinking: mid '50s.
Cause of sinking: probable collision
        with reef or explosion on board.
Site position: on the shore side of the
        reef at Zabargad.
Distance from shore: a few metres.
Minimum depth: emerging from
        the surface.
Maximum depth: 24 metres.

THE CARGO BOAT
AT ZABARGAD

Very little is known about the large cargo vessel (about 70 metres in length) which went down just off the island of Zabargad some forty or fifty years ago. The fact that it sank on the leeward side of the reef suggests that some incident - a sudden engine failure, for instance - may have led it to seek shelter here, away from the force of the currents.

As the ship manoeuvred on the inner side of the reef, its starboard flank very probably collided with the coral bank and it sprang two leaks: a smaller one towards the stern and a very large one in the bows. But this is only one of many guesses that can be made about how the vessel met its sad fate. According to other sources, the bigger of the two holes was caused by an explosion that occurred when the ship was already on the leeward side of the reef, where it attempted to find an emergency anchorage; the hole certainly looks as though it could have been caused by an explosion.

The material damage is unchallengeable evidence of the vessel's tragic end but there are no clues to its identity and history. We know only that it met the same fate as many other ships which have sunk in mysterious circumstances, often without their name ever being discovered.

The lifeboats are still a chilling reminder of the drama that surely surrounded the last moments of the Zabargad cargo ship. Instants after the collision with the reef, the anchors must have been dropped and the lifeboats lowered (they were of the English, pump-operated type): two ended up on the beach in front of the wreck; a third ran aground on the opposite side of the island. And they have remained there ever since.

A

B

C

A - A diver hovers above the bow of the boat where, thanks to the transparent water, various parts and fittings can be clearly seen: the capstan from which the anchors were hoisted, two large bitts and some lines left on the deck. Visible in the background, to the left, is the open door of one of the hatchways leading to the forecastle.
Photograph by Claudio Ziraldo

B - Concretionary growths are still few in the stern section too and rails, bitts and capstan can be examined in every detail; in the bottom left-hand corner is part of the companionway leading up to the bridge.
Photograph by Claudio Ziraldo

C - Pictured here is a diver close to one of the lifeboat davits; although there is no sure account of exactly how and why this freighter sank, very probably no lives were lost.
Photograph by Claudio Ziraldo

Diving to the wreck

The vessel now lies at a depth of 24 metres. The strong tides that sweep this stretch of the Red Sea have had destructive effects on the wreck: over the years the bow section took severe battering and eventually rolled right over onto its port flank.
Finding the wreck is fairly simple since the main mast still emerges from the water; your cover boat can therefore be moored close to the exact site. All the same, it is advisable to make the dive only when weather conditions are very good, with calm seas and clear water.
By far the best time of day for the dive is early afternoon, when the light is at its best.
This wreck may appear to offer little of interest but divers actually have some exciting moments in store for them during the exploration.
You can start in the stern which gives access to the engine room - divided into three compartments -,

D

D - Although the vessel has already been lying on the seabed for several decades, its structures have remained almost intact in the exceptionally limpid water and practically free of encrustation; as a result the wreck has an amazingly surreal look.
Photograph by Massimo Bicciato

E - Pointing up towards the surface is one of the masts, fixed to which were a derrick (one of its pulleys can still be seen) and sidelights.
Photograph by Claudio Ziraldo

E

F

G

and then make your way upwards to the bridge. Among the areas to visit on the main deck is the captain's cabin, where you can still see the telephone, radio station and the space formerly occupied by the course plotting table. In the forepart of the ship you will notice four hatchways: these lead to rooms used for

stores, where there are some boxes containing metal parts and spares for the engine.
It is nonetheless presumed that - on what was destined to be its last voyage - the vessel was also carrying cargo; since the holds are now practically empty, it is probable that plunderers have removed anything of value.

F - A diver hovers just above a well-preserved companionway; with so much of interest to explore, the dive to the Zabargad cargo boat is always a fascinating experience.
Photograph by Claudio Ziraldo

G - Still visible on the bridge are a number of navigation instruments, including the magnetic compass to be found on every ship.
Photograph by Massimo Bicciato

A

A - The main mast stretches up towards the surface and emerges above the water, making it very easy to locate the site of the sunken freighter. Photograph by Claudio Ziraldo

B - Some surgeonfish swim near an air duct; the wreck provides shelter for countless different species. Photograph by Vincenzo Paolillo

While exploring the ship's interiors, take care to move cautiously: you can very easily kick up clouds of suspended particles, reducing visibility. The stern section is a diver's delight: as well as exploring the interior of the wreck, you can feast your eyes on an incredible abundance of marine life and the spectacular colours typical of the underwater world of the Red Sea.
Don't miss this chance to admire and take great photographs of the windlasses now colonized by soft and hard corals, and the many dangling cables on which colourful alcyonarians grow in profusion.

B

D

D - The exceptionally well-preserved structures and machines of the Zabargad freighter make it well worth exploring in detail; while doing so, great care must be taken not to stir up the thick layer of sediment, which would otherwise spoil part of the enjoyment of the dive. Photograph by Massimo Bicciato

E - Several hatches in the stern area give access to the machine room, divided by watertight bulkheads into three adjoining rooms: here the darkness and notable risk of suspended sediment means only experienced divers should make their way in. Photograph by Massimo Bicciato

C

C - Many of the ship's fittings are still visible on the deck: for instance, this spool on which a fire hose was probably once wound. Photograph by Massimo Bicciato

E

F - The port anchor chain hanging from the hawsehole indicates that the ship did not sink immediately after its collision with the reef, since the crew had time to attempt an emergency mooring.
Photograph by Vincenzo Paolillo

G - The bridge - like the rest of the wreck - is still more or less intact, its porthole windows still in place.
Photograph by Vincenzo Paolillo

H - A thick metal cable lies abandoned on the foredeck, looking almost as though it were about to be picked up and used again.
Photograph by Vincenzo Paolillo

I - Inside the bridge itself one can still see the fairly well-preserved control boards of the ship's electrical systems.
Photograph by Massimo Bicciato

J - A feature worth examining on the bridge is a gimbaled magnetic compass, its glass cover still perfectly transparent.
Photograph by Massimo Bicciato

K - Through a rent in the floor of the bridge, divers can easily spot the rudder wheel.
Photograph by Vincenzo Paolillo

F

G
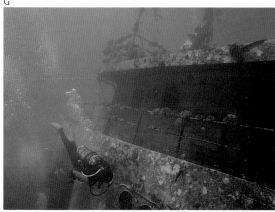

H
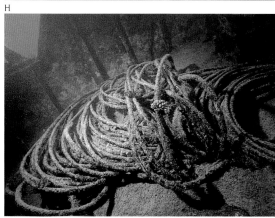

I

J

K

BLUE BELL
by Andrea Ghisotti

SAUDI ARABIA
EGYPT
RED SEA
SUDAN
ERITREA
YEMEN

SUDAN
▼ *BLUE BELL*
● PORT SUDAN

RATINGS

Finding site: easy.
Visibility: excellent.
Current: weak to moderate.
Dive difficulty: medium to difficult.
Presence of lines and nets: none.
Historical interest: low.
Photographic interest: high.
Biological interest: medium.

DATA FILE

Type of wreck: cargo ship.
Nationality: unknown.
Year of construction: unknown.
Tonnage: 7,000 tons (estimated).
Date of sinking: end of '70s.
Cause of sinking: collision with reef.
Geographical coordinates:
      37°17.50'N, 20°13.20'E.
Site position: close to Sha'ab Su'adi
      reef.
Distance from shore: against
the reef.
Minimum depth: 20 metres.
Maximum depth: 90 metres.

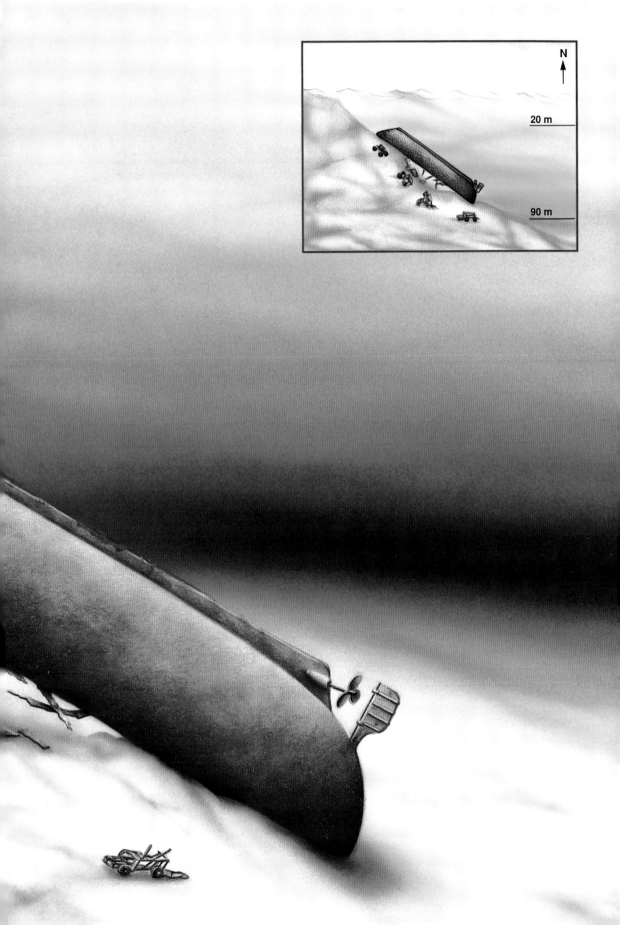

THE CARGO BOAT *BLUE BELL*

North of Port Sudan, rising close to the surface of the water from great depths (500-700 metres), are a series of reefs teeming with marine life and considered among the most stupendous in the whole Red Sea. Their names - which include Sanganeb and Sha'ab Rumi - have now become legendary and they have the added advantage of being only a few hours away by boat. Slightly further north, about 35-40 miles from Port Sudan, there is another huge reef called Sha'ab Su'adi. It is between 2 and 7 miles from a point on the coast where there is a small lagoon - a "marsa", as they are called around these parts - a favourite haunt of numerous birds (including fisher hawk, which build their characteristic circular nests here). There are also a few wooden huts at Marsa Arakiyai, home to a small military unit which keeps watch on navigation and smuggling, of which there is plenty along the Sudanese coast. After heading out to sea from the small landing-stage, you are soon within reach of the reef and, as you approach it, you notice a tangle of rusty metal in the midst of a coral formation emerging from the water. It is an old *Toyota*. How it came to be perched on an isolated reef in the middle of the Red Sea is not immediately obvious. The explanation is to be found beneath the surface, on the outer wall of reef, for here lies the gigantic wreck of the *Blue Bell*. The cargo ship went aground on the reef in the second half of the '70s while carrying a full load of *Toyota* vehicles (which is why it is generally known as "the *Toyota* wreck"). How this huge ship finished up on the reef is a complete mystery. The shipping routes through the Red Sea pass much further out, in the central channel, at a safe distance from the perilous reefs that hug the coastline. What's more, the ship is lying in a strange position, at right-angles to the reef and to the shore, as though it has been coming from the coast of Saudi Arabia. Could it have been trying to reach the coast

A - As this picture of the bow clearly shows, the wreck of the Blue Bell *lies completely overturned on the seabed, at a depth between 20 and 25 metres.*
Photograph by Andrea Ghisotti

B - The entire cargo of the Blue Bell *was made up of* Toyota *vehicles, their buckled remains now dotted around the wreck on the sea floor, often in the weirdest positions.*
Photograph by Andrea Ghisotti

C - A scuba diver takes a look at one of the Toyota pick-ups from the cargo of the Blue Bell: *it may have been when attempting to smuggle vehicles ashore that the ship collided with the reef.*
Photograph by Andrea Ghisotti

D - A huge six-axle truck lies upside-down on top of another identical one (right) and the remains of a pick-up (left), the cab of which is almost totally destroyed.
Photograph by Andrea Ghisotti

at that particular point, in order to moor in the tiny Marsa Arakiyai and secretly unload the vehicles it had on board? In theory this would be possible since, some 20-30 metres north of the wreck site, there is a break in the Sha'ab Su'adi reef and a pass 35 metres deep; the"marsa" too offers a means of reaching the shore. Whatever the case, the ship must have struck the reef with considerable force, since one of the cars was thrown from the deck right onto the reef. Some heavy trucks, four-wheel drives, saloons and pick-ups stand normally, with their wheels resting firmly on the seabed, others are completely upside-down; some are instead suspended from tackle or balance on their front- or tail-end, supported by wreckage or by the wall of the reef. Towering over this "submarine breaker's yard" the huge hulk of the *Blue Bell* lies overturned on the seabed, her keel facing upwards and her enormous bow pointing towards the reef.

Diving to the wreck

In itself the dive is not particularly difficult, provided you limit your visit to the stem of the ship and the vehicles scattered around it. Here the water is 20-25 metres deep and it is generally beautifully clear, with the possibility of current on windy days. It is fun to try and identify the models of the vehicles, checking out their various features. As always the tyres have best stood the passage of time underwater, but the batteries and some of the plastic trim show little sign of concretion. The hull of the ship is imposing but it has few distinctive elements since all the superstructures have been crushed between the deck and seafloor and are therefore inexplorable. As you make your way along the forward part of the keel, you can see the gaping hole that caused the ship to sink. More experienced divers can continue along the flank to the point where there is a sudden vertical drop in the reef, from a depth of 30-35 metres down to 50. Here the vessel is not right against the bottom and its structures are plainly visible. A great artificial tunnel has been created between wreck and seafloor. As the water forces its way through this

E

G

F

E - It is clear from this photograph that the tyres have survived the corrosive effects of the salt water.
Photograph by Andrea Ghisotti

F - Shown here are the remains of the cab of one of the Toyota vehicles: the metal structures are now thick with concretions but the parts made from plastic are still hardly touched.
Photograph by Vincenzo Paolillo

G - From the starboard hawsehole hangs the remaining anchor, with its bills oddly pointing downwards due to the position of the vessel.
Photograph by Vincenzo Paolillo

channel, the current gets stronger and carries larger quantities of nourishment. This has encouraged profuse growth of cnidarian species, especially soft corals that reach an incredible size. Another astonishing sight are the carcasses of a few vehicles which, crushed and deformed by the collision, now hang from the ship like Christmas decorations. Diving in this area of the ship presents more risks and you had best continue no further, even if it would be possible to pass through the "tunnel" to the other side of the ship, slip between the trapped vehicles and even reach the holds. But the depth and dimensions of the ship make further exploration inadvisable, and the same goes for the descent towards the stern, where the rudder and single huge central

screw are prominent features. Here the depth is already at least 70 metres and where the stern rests on the sea bed, it is between 85 and 90 metres, far too deep! Remember too that these parts of the ship are quite a distance from the bow and you can't make a vertical ascent to re-surface, far from the reef and your cover boat. Night dives to this wreck are not recommended: the pass is situated slightly north of a point considered one of the best places in the Sudanese Red Sea to catch large sharks. An Italian film crew who wanted to shoot some pictures with sharks was brought to this very spot by Nabir, captain of the *Felicidad*, who left bait in the pass. During the night a mako, a real monster of a shark, fell for the bait but the next morning was itself torn to pieces by a smaller tiger shark.

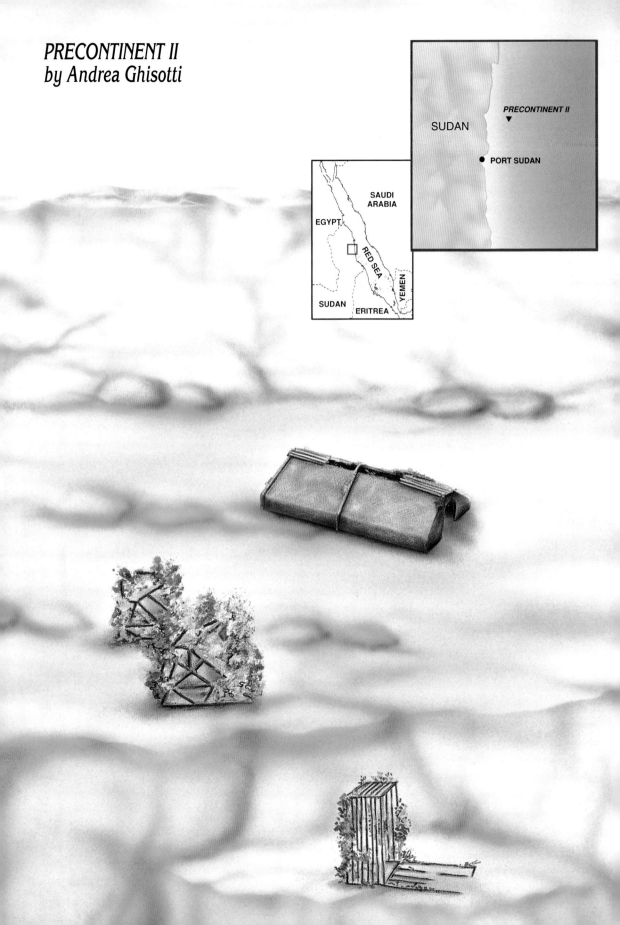

PRECONTINENT II
by Andrea Ghisotti

SUDAN

PRECONTINENT II

● PORT SUDAN

SAUDI
ARABIA

EGYPT

RED SEA

YEMEN

SUDAN

ERITREA

RATINGS

Finding site: easy.
Visibility: excellent.
Current: weak.
Dive difficulty: easy to medium.
Presence of lines and nets: none.
Historical interest: high.
Photographic interest: high.
Biological interest: high.

DATA FILE

Type of wreck: underwater scientific
      research village.
Year of construction: 1963.
Geographical coordinates:
      37°24'N, 19°55.45'E.
Site position: west side of Sha'ab
      Rumi reef.
Distance from shore: a few metres.
Minimum depth: 7 metres.
Maximum depth: 45 metres.

PRECONTINENT II

It was just about midday when, on September 14, 1962, Albert Falco and Claude Wesly pulled on their diving masks and plunged into the sea. This was the start of *Precontinent I*, the first experiment in underwater living long dreamed of by Captain Jacques Cousteau and now at last reality. The site chosen for the experiment was the island of Pomègue, off Marseilles. Here a large pontoon had been anchored to the seafloor at a depth of 12 metres, to provide the base for a small submarine chamber, 5 metres long and 2.44 metres high. For two weeks this was to be "home" to the two divers, who would breathe air at an atmospheric pressure of 2 bar, double that of outside pressure, and do five hours' work a day.

The experiment was a complete success: it was proved that man can live beneath the ocean without problems, with a single recompression phase at the end of the period spent underwater. A year later, in 1963, the second step in the conquest of submarine space began. This time no fewer than eight men were to spend a month underwater, again at a depth of 10-12 metres, while two of them were to descend deeper to spend a week in a base anchored at 26 metres. Organizing *Precontinent II* was a far more complicated business because the chosen site was not on the seafloor of home waters but in the midst of the Red Sea, at the Sha'ab Rumi reef, 22 miles from Port Sudan and 9 miles from shore. Nobody who does not know this part of the world can fully understand what organizing a submarine village here involved. Even today, thirty years on, finding a stainless steel bolt in Port Sudan is no mean task, and getting to an airport in time to catch a plane still requires careful planning and a lot of luck. But no finer site could have been chosen. The Sha'ab Rumi reef is one of the richest marine environments in Sudan, long and narrow with a

A

B

A - The dome-shaped structure used as a hangar is the most striking remaining feature of what was once the site of Precontinent II, the submarine village designed by Jacques Cousteau and built in 1963 for scientific research purposes.

B - Inspiration for the design of the hangar of the Soucoupe plongeante *clearly came from the global external shell of a sea urchin (without spines, of course); once painted yellow, the metal plates are now thickly encrusted with hard coral.*

beautiful lagoon in its midst, where the *Calypso* was able to remain safely anchored for the whole period of the experiment. Also part of the expedition was the Italian ship *Rosaldo*, with its Sicilian crew: on board this floating base were huge compressors, generators and many other necessary items of equipment. A walkway across the reef was installed, to make it easier to move between the open sea and the lagoon. The location chosen for the village was beside the external wall of the reef, very close to the

pass into the lagoon; it was an ideal site since it had a flat "terrace" - sufficiently wide to accommodate the small village - before dropping to much greater depths. All the structures were brought from Europe. They were fixed to the bottom with steel cables and stays and were blocked in position with 200 tons of lead. The village was comprised of a series of prefabricated buildings which, even in their exterior design, reflected their marine setting. The most important was Starfish

House where the exploration team lived. It had five rooms: a central chamber and four "arms".
The living quarters had most of the "mod cons" generally found in an apartment - shower and W.C., bunk beds, chairs and tables, stereo system plus - of course - comprehensive instrumentation, including TV-cameras able to monitor the village and the ships on the surface. The second building - resembling a giant sea urchin - was the hangar of the *Soucoupe Plongeante*, the tiny disk-shaped bathyscaphe used to descend to a depth of 300 metres. The hangar was a large shell, full of air, its bottom open to allow the *Soucoupe* to slip inside and subsequently be winched up out of the water. The bathyscaphe ventured out on many explorations during those weeks but never surfaced. Mechanics and technicians instead went down to the hangar where, in a dry environment but breathing air with an atmospheric pressure of 2 bar, they carried out maintenance, recharged batteries, changed gas cylinders and reloaded film in the cameras. The third building was a shed for tools; the underwater scooters were kept in this long, narrow greenhouse-like structure, together with all the everyday working equipment needed by the divers. Lastly there was the deep submersible cabin, in which two members of the team spent an entire week. It was comprised of two rooms, one on top of the other: the lower one communicated directly with the water and here the divers got out of their scuba gear and showered. Accommodation in the tiny "upstairs" room was necessarily much more spartan than in the spacious "house" closer to the surface. Even deeper, at 51 metres, there was a cage for sharks, and others were put along the whole length of the reef cliff; they could be closed with gates and were fitted with an alarm connected with the surface. Completing the village was the so-called fish corral, a kind of acquarium of intriguing, futuristic design, constructed with a series of triangular glazed elements.

C

D

C - A scuba diver approaches the remains of the "fish corral", the curious acquarium made from triangular glazed elements where Cousteau's team kept specimens of fish they intended to study.

D - Spectacular growths of hard corals and alcyionarians cover the abandoned structures of Precontinent II, the underwater village in which eight oceanauts spent a whole month in 1963.

The various services needed by the 8 men living below the surface were performed by 25 other divers: these included daily cleaning of the outside walls, to remove seaweed which grew incredibly fast.
The routine followed in the village was not unlike everyday life in a seaside village on shore, with alternating periods of work and sleep. Small fishing nets had been placed in the area and one of the men's jobs was to check them periodically: fish caught were placed in see-through plastic bags and plexiglas containers - where they came under heavy attack from predators like snappers, morays and groupers - before being transferred to the fish corral. On other occasions samples of coral were collected, excursions were made in the *Soucoupe*, new areas were explored and filmed and - less fun - there were medical check-ups. It was found that, during the first few days underwater, the high partial pressure of oxygen in the air the men breathed (the main "house"

was at a depth of 11 metres) caused a decrease in red corpuscles, after which levels stabilized; this is the reverse of the situation encountered when time is spent above a certain height in the mountains. In addition each of the eight men had to spend 10 minutes a day under a UV lamp, to make up for the lack of sunlight.

A complete laboratory for biological field research was installed in Starfish House: it was the first ever of its kind in which organisms could be studied immediately after capture, without reducing ambient pressure; no such possibility existed above the surface. Meals were taken down in large pressure cookers and the ship's cook did his very best to produce appetizing food that would help keep morale high underwater. One day the ship's parrot was taken down inside a pressure cooker... he adapted very well to his new surroundings, staring curiously at the fish swimming past the large window. The divers could venture out for up to 5 hours at 25 metres, or shorter spells at depths of even 50 metres. In the deep cabin, at 26 metres, air was replaced by a mixture of nitrogen, helium and oxygen; the large filter used to absorb carbon dioxide (50 kilos of soda lime) had to be changed every two days. The operational depth for the two divers based in this cabin was 50 metres, with occasional short descents to 100-110 metres. After a week at this depth they had to breathe a high-oxygen mixture for three hours before returning for good to Starfish House, their special mission successfully completed. *Precontinent II* paved the way for the conquest of the underwater world: much that is now considered routine in the area of deep-water oceanographic research has its roots in this extraordinary experiment, conducted thirty years ago.

A - A diver examines the coral-encrusted remains of the tools shed; Cousteau used the underwater village as the set for his documentary film "World without Sunlight".

B - Several cages to trap sharks were put along the wall of the reef, close to the village; abandoned at the end of the experiment, the cages are now covered with concretions.

Diving to the wreck

When Jacques Cousteau returned to the *Precontinent II* site for a visit four years later, he found the remaining buildings still in an excellent condition, although colonies of hard corals already covered much of the structures. Thirty years on, the remains of the village are still standing; they are now increasingly mantled but not yet masked by coral growths which heighten their visual appeal.

At the end of the experiment the two "houses", full of expensive equipment, were dismantled and retrieved; on the site remain the hangar, tools shed, fish corral and various shark cages, as well as piles of cables, beams, metal sections and assorted scrap.

For any diver who knows the history of *Precontinent II*, exploring its remains is a fascinating but emotionally draining experience, much like wandering around a Gold Rush ghost town. The hangar of the *Soucoupe* in particular has a vaguely lunar look, its sea urchin body perched on the "legs" through which it is still easy to obtain access to the interior. Once you have passed through the usual wall of silvery fish, you can rise to the air bubble - occasionally replenished with the exhaust bubbles of visiting divers -, emerge above the surface, remove your mask and regulator and say a few words, which echo strangely around the empty space.

On your left, looking seaward, there are now two wonderful great mushroom coral formations which have joined to create a tablelike mass. On the right is the tools shed, still well conserved but not nearly so picturesque. All around, encrusted with coral, are the old cables which held the buildings to the seabed. Nabir, a former captain of the *Felicidad*, a charter boat based at Port Sudan, worked here in 1963, preparing the site for the expedition. For three months he chummed the area, attracting an infinite variety of fish to create more interesting scenery for "World without Sunlight", the documentary filmed by the Cousteau team during the *Precontinent II* experiment.

According to Nabir, the area was then frequented by incredible numbers of sharks, snappers and surgeonfish.

There are still plenty of fish here but it is worth moving towards nearby South Point if you want to see the local fauna at its best. Slightly further away from the other structures are the remains of the fish corral: this already strange construction is now clad in a mantle of fanciful, brightly coloured concretions, with sponges and alcyonarians among the most prominent decorative features. The first shark cage is deeper down, at 30 metres, and there is another at around 40-45 metres; descend to this one first, so you can dispel some of the nitrogen during the second part of the dive.

C - A diver "shelters" for a moment beneath the huge umbrella of stony coral that now forms a kind of roof over one side of the hangar; a similar, slightly smaller formation can be seen on the left.

D - Inside, the top part of the hangar is still watertight and there is a huge air bubble, replenished with the exhaust bubbles of visiting divers who can even remove their mask and exchange a few words.

All the photos of the dive to Precontinent II were taken by Andrea Ghisotti.

UMBRIA
by Andrea Ghisotti

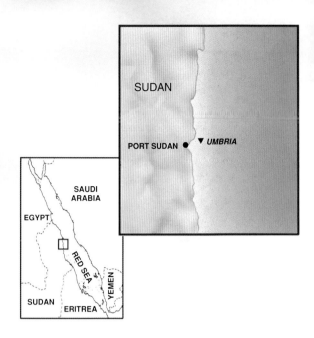

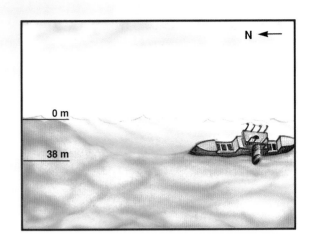

RATINGS

Finding site: easy.
Visibility: fairly good.
Current: weak to moderate,
Dive difficulty: medium to difficult.
Presence of lines and nets: none.
Historical interest: high.
Photographic interest: high.
Biological interest: high.

DATA FILE

Type of wreck: cargo-passenger ship.
Nationality: Italian.
Year of construction: 1911
Tonnage: 10,128 tons.
Date of sinking: 10/6/1940.
Cause of sinking: scuttled,
Site position: against Wingate Reef.
Geographical coordinates:
         37°19.40'N, 19°38.20'E.
Distance from shore: 200 metres
         from reef.
Minimum depth: emerging from
         the surface.
Maximum depth: 38 metres.

The motorship *Umbria* was launched in the Reiherst Schiffswerke shipyard in Hamburg on December 30, 1911, commissioned by Hamburg Amerika Linie. Its name was then *Bahia Blanca*, a reference to the routes to South America - and primarily Argentina - which was in fact the ship's destination for many years. By March 1912 it was ready to put out to sea. It was a big ship: 155 metres long and 18 wide, able to carry 2,400 passengers in two classes, with a gross tonnage of 10,128 tons; it had five boilers but only one funnel supplying steam to two triple-expansion alternating engines which produced 4,300 horsepower and gave the vessel a cruising speed of 12 knots. At the outbreak of World War I it was blocked and interned in the port of Buenos Aires, where it remained until 1918 when it was sold to the Argentine government, who used it until 1935. It was then taken out of commission and bought by the Italian government who put it in the charge of the Genoa-based Italia shipping line. It was renamed *Umbria* and refitted for use as a troopship; as such it made a total of 16 runs to Italian colonies in East Africa. Quarters for 129 officers were provided in the midship section and berths for 2,168 soldiers elsewhere in the vessel, even in the holds. Sold on January 1, 1937 to Lloyd Triestino, the *Umbria* was used on routes to Spain, Libya and Cyrenaica, Albania and Eritrea.

The *Umbria* began her last voyage in the ports of Genoa, Leghorn and Naples, where her holds were packed with huge quantities of munitions destined for troops stationed in Italy's East African colonies. It seems unbelievable, since Italy was on the point of entering the war, but loading was carried out in broad daylight, "while nannies pushed perambulators up and down the dockside", as I was told by Captain Lorenzo Muiesan, a native of

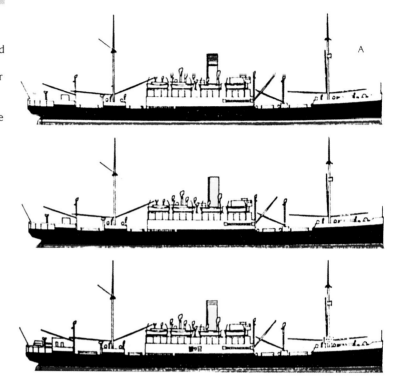

Trieste, born in 1895, whom I had the good fortune to interview face to face. The ship had undoubtedly been entrusted with a very important cargo, indispensable for an army at war: 360,000 bombs (the equivalent of 6,000 tons) and 60 boxes of detonators and incendiary devices. The rest of the cargo - for a total weight of 8,487.5 tons - was comprised of bags of cement, building materials and assorted goods of the sort that ships usually carry. After a last call at Messina to take on fuel, on May 28, 1940 the ship set off for

A - These three drawings show how the appearance of the ship changed from 1935 onwards, when it sailed as the Umbria (it was first launched in 1911 with the name Bahia Blanca). Above: the Umbria in 1935, fitted out to carry troops to Africa; centre: the Umbria in 1937, used by Lloyd

Triestino on the Mediterranean routes; below: the Umbria in 1940, with the Italian flag painted on the sides of the bridge deck, fitted out as a supplies ship for troops in Italy's East African colonies. Photograph by Andrea Ghisotti, printed with kind permission of the Associazione Marinara Aldebaran

Massaua and Aden, the two Red Sea ports which were the destination of much of its cargo, after which it was to sail on to Calcutta, its ultimate destination. On June 3, at Port Said, it took on 1,000 tons of coal and 130 of water. The following morning 23 men of the Royal Navy came on board, with 2 pilots, and together they succeeded in making the descent of the Suez Canal, which normally took three hours, exasperatingly slow. The British, informed of Italy's imminent entry into the war and well aware of what the ship was carrying, were anxious to get their hands on the cargo. Two days passed before the "guests" disembarked and only on June 6 was the *Umbria* able to continue south, at speed. But the Royal Navy sloop *Grimsby* was close behind. Muiesan telegraphed ahead to Massaua: "There's a ship on my trail, be prepared". At 7.30 a.m. on June 9, when the *Umbria* was just off Port Sudan, she was stopped by the *Grimsby* with the excuse of a "contraband control", and was forced to anchor by Wingate Reef. Anchors with seven lengths of chain (175 metres) were lowered, with 25 metres of water beneath the bow and 40 beneath the stern. The *Umbria* was carrying a full load and drew 28 foot (about 9 metres). Before long the New Zealand battle-cruiser *Leander* arrived at the scene from Port Sudan and Lieutenant Stevens, with a group of 22 men, boarded the *Umbria*. They brought their own rations and bedded down for the night on the Italian ship. Morning broke on June 10, later to prove a fateful day. The first few hours passed uneventfully: Stevens was playing for time, Muiesan was getting impatient. He had the deck washed down (it had got dirty when loading coal) and, on returning to his cabin to wash his hands, turned the radio on. At that very moment the programme was interrupted to broadcast a communiqué from Radio Addis Abeba: "Calling all troups of the empire. War will be declared at 19.00 hours, fighting will commence at midnight". Muiesan was dumbstruck. He had been

expecting it but now he had to act fast, in the hope that the British had not yet heard the news. He called Danilo, his twenty-year-old orderly, and handed him a bundle of segret documents and confidential papers: "Burn them in the galley stove and send the first officer to me right away". When Zarli arrived, he told him of the turn of events and instructed him to tell Costa, the chief engineer, to do his best to sink the ship, naturally without letting the British realize what was going on. But Costa wanted nothing to do with it: "...but this stuff is worth a fortune, we can't do it!" Meanwhile Muiesan had to devise some way to save all his men. He sent Zarli to Stevens, asking for permission to hold an "abandon ship" drill, Stevens luckily made no objection. "But what is Costa up to?"

A few tremendously tense moments passed. Then the two British soldiers on guard at the holds ran to tell Stevens that huge quantities of water were pouring in. Marcorini and Isiacic, the two saboteurs, had done the job properly: using a sledge hammer, they had split

open the two iron rings connected to the main sea cocks, as well as to the secondary one and the watertight door of the shaft tunnel, creating openings about half a metre in diameter. Muiesan realized his plan had succeeded and gave the real order to abandon ship. It was supper time and a mouthwatering smell of sauce for a tasty dish of pasta was already spreading from the galley: the crew grumbled as they lowered the lifeboats. Stevens came rushing to the scene, demanding explanations. "Italy has entered the war and I have scuttled my ship", replied Muiesan. For a moment Stevens lost his English sang-froid, stamped his foot and became red in the face; but seconds later he regained his self-control and he too gave the order to abandon ship. Soon only the two of them remained on board and, courteous to the last, neither wanted to be the first to descend into the lifeboat, although the ship was now listing. So Muiesan said: "No, you must go first, I am your prisoner", at which Stevens, moved by the Italian captain's gesture, replied: "No, you are my friend!" The captain of the *Grimsby* wanted to question Muiesan. "What have you done to your ship?" he asked, and he looked him straight in the eye knowing full well that, had the *Umbria* been mined, all the explosives in its holds would cause a bloodbath. "I have only scuttled the ship" replied Muiesan. "Nothing else?" "Nothing else". "I believe you" said the captain, and he shook Muiesan's hand. While, now on board the *Leander*, the officers and crew of the *Umbria* - 77 men in all - were being provided with a meal, a sailor rushed up, closed the hatch and, amid the general excitement, broke the news: it was official, Italy had entered the war. The ship returned to Port Sudan and the Italians were put in a shed under a sheet-metal roof. It was June and, with a temperature of 50 degrees in the shed, the heat was unbearable. As they started five long years as prisoners-of-war, the Italians were joined by an unexpected companion: the ship's cat which, in the confusion, had

A

A - The bows of the *Umbria* are high and tapered, the typical shape of ships built in the early years of this century. 155 metres long and 18 wide, the Italian steamship had a gross tonnage of 10,128 tons. With its five boilers, it reached a cruising speed of 12 knots.
Photograph by Andrea Ghisotti

B - Two scuba divers descend to explore the bridge deck; two lifeboat davits can be seen behind them. This part of the wreck is lavishly endowed with huge formations of hard coral; swimming all around is an amazing assortment of the many marine creatures to be found in the Red Sea.
Photograph by Andrea Ghisotti

B

C - Still in place along the starboard flank, now colonized by sponges and splendid hard corals, are the delicate-looking railings; only limited damage has been done to them by erosion and pounding waves.
Photograph by Andrea Ghisotti

D - A bright red sponge adds a pleasing note of colour to the starboard railings. The exceptional state of conservation of the wreck and the abundance of marine flora and fauna make the dive to the Umbria *an unforgettable experience.*
Photograph by Franco Banfi

E - This diver looks minute beside the still visible enormous starboard screw; the port screw is instead now buried under the mud.
Photograph by Andrea Ghisotti

F - A diver peers into the opening of a huge air duct which, with the wreck sloping at such an angle, is now directed upwards.
Photograph by Andrea Ghisotti

got left on board. Having spotted the poor creature crouching on one of the lifeboat davits, miraculously still above water, a small English party had gone to rescue it.

The presence of the *Umbria* was a source of considerable concern. Salvaging the vessel would not have been difficult but, with all those explosives on board, it was decided to leave well alone.

After the war the British sent their bomb disposal experts who estimated that, in the event of an explosion, half Port Sudan would have ended up under water. An order strictly forbidding anyone to approach the wreck was issued.

In 1949 Hans Hass appeared on the scene. A celebrated pioneer of underwater exploration, this Austrian had amazed the world with his underwater pictures and tales of close encounters with sharks, shortly before the war.

He arrived alone, bringing with him just a *Leica* in a DIY housing and a 16 mm film-camera, a harpoon (just in case...), breathing apparatus and... his dinner jacket for receptions at the embassy. As soon as he heard about the *Umbria*, ban or no ban, he decided to explore the wreck. The *Umbria* was resting on her port flank, with a marked list: only a small section of her masts now emerged from the water, providing a convenient perch for the birds which had covered them in snow-white guano. Descending with his breathing apparatus and his faithful *Leica* in its housing, Hass took a series of wonderful black and white photographs, but managed to flood his camera at the first dive.

Everything on board was absolutely intact, just as it had been left in such haste - nine years before. The ship's structures were already extensively encrusted with large hard coral outgrowths whereas the cargo, shut in the holds, had few surface concretions. Many years ago, when I dived to the *Umbria* for the first time, I made a fascinating discovery. I was nearing the end of my dive and my lamp had practically run out. A small torch lent by a co-diver produced a dim light and with this, I ventured into a hold which I

117

A - Relatively free of concretions, the gigantic rudder is a thrilling sight in the exploration of the Umbria, its pintles and arms still clearly discernible. Photograph by Andrea Ghisotti

B - Still visible on the sea floor, at a depth of 35 metres, is one of the lifeboats which sank at the same time as the ship. Photograph by Andrea Ghisotti

C - Not far from the stern on the starboard side is a small, metal handbasin: adding a striking note of colour to the photo are a threadfin butterfly fish, centre, and a striped butterfly fish, below. Photograph by Andrea Ghisotti

had not yet explored, squeezing past part of the cargo which partly blocked the entrance. As I tried to find my way in the dark, the light from the torch suddenly caught a huge steel eye, staring in my direction: it was the headlamp of a car or truck, I could not make out which because at that very moment the torch went out too and I was left in semi-darkness, struggling to find my way out. I returned to the wreck the following year and searched for the vehicle again but initially I covered the length and breadth of the ship and hunted in every hold in vain. I was on the point of giving up

D - On the bridge deck, more extensively damaged than other parts of the ship, concretions and other forms of underwater life are now well-established; the handsome fish at the centre of the photo is a splendid angelfish. Photograph by Andrea Ghisotti

when I noticed a space, in front of the quarter-deck, that I had previously missed. And sure enough, my torch illuminated not one but three splendid '30s cars, neatly lined up and covered with a fascinating layer of greenish-yellow concretions. Before my exhaust bubbles stuck to the ceiling above, sending down clouds of sediment, I managed to take photos and peer into the cars' interior: there were three rows of seats - upholstery and padding long gone - and I could clearly see the dashboard with its simple instrumentation, gear stick, steering wheel and other details. On returning to Italy I was determined to find out the model. As the design of the vertical radiator had struck me as typically Fiat, I got in touch with the

Archives department of the *Fiat Motor Company* in Turin, where Antonio Amadelli proved an expert and enthusiastic collaborator. Our first attempts at identifying the model took place by phone: with the photos in a viewer, I tried to spot details with a magnifying glass while Amadelli, at the other end of the line, reeled off questions: "... Can you see a bead on the bonnet? Do the front windows have a vent window?" We narrowed the possible models down to two: the *Fiat 1100 Lunghe* or the *2800*. I mailed the photos to Turin and, a few days later, received official confirmation: it was the *Fiat 1100 Lunghe*, the six-seater version of a top-selling car produced between '39 and '48, in this case probably the colonial version with its distinctive tyre-tread.

Diving to the wreck

The *Umbria* has a length of 150 metres and a single dive can convey only a superficial idea of the ship. This may be enough for anyone only mildly interested in wrecks but real enthusiasts will want to make a number of dives, making new discoveries with each visit. It rarely happens that a sunken ship is completely intact, without signs of bombardments or collisions, and with the bonus of a full, varied and interesting cargo. After some fifty-five years on the sea floor, damage is still contained and limited essentially to the bridge, which is still only just below the surface and so exposed to the swell. The masts have collapsed and rest on the bottom together with the loading booms; so has the funnel which now lies at a slant. The central part of the ship can even be explored without breathing apparatus and there is much to be said for getting a general impression of the wreck with just mask and fins. The bridge structures are slightly damaged but you still get a good idea of this section of the ship, with the four pairs of lifeboat davits on each flank, the large cylindrical hole where the funnel was and the rooms just a few metres underwater, which you can peer

E

E - This fine archive photograph is of a Fiat 1100 Lunga, a popular six-seater vehicle made by the Turin-based motor manufacturer from 1939 to 1948. As well as huge quantities of munitions, deep in the holds of the Umbria *are three* Fiat 1100 Lunga *cars, undoubtedly meant for Italy's African colonies.* Photograph by Andrea Ghisotti

F, G - The cars on board the Umbria *were probably fitted out for use in the colonies, with filters to stop sand getting into the carburetor and sprayed with matte glare-preventing paint; they also had tyres with corrugated tread, for driving on desert terrain.* Photographs by Andrea Ghisotti

F

G

instead sunk almost completely into the mud. Close to the handrail, on the starboard flank, you will notice a small, metal handbasin. The holds are located between the stern and the bridge: none of them has covers and so access is fairly easy. Pay attention all the same to suspended particles and to the cargo, which is in many cases precariously balanced on the starboard side and could collapse. The quantity of munitions contained in the wreck is awesome. There are entire holds packed with hundreds of neatly stacked high-explosive bombs, others full of boxes with bomb rudders and detonators.

It must not be forgotten that risks

B - Pictured in this photograph is the dashboard of one of the cars; unfortunately, the steering wheel is not in place anymore, may be taken as the souvenir of a diver's grabbing raid. Photograph by Andrea Ghisotti

B

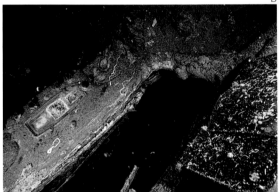

A - The distinctive radiator of one of the three Fiat 1100 Lunga cars can be seen in this close-up; thanks to this particular feature it was eventually possible to identify the exact model of the vehicles. Photograph by Andrea Ghisotti

into through portholes on the starboard side. Corals and fish are plentiful in this area. The fish which have made the *Umbria* their home are used to divers and let them come to close quarters, almost posing for photographs.

Equipped with scuba gear, start your dive from the stern, first finning back a few metres to get a panoramic view. The stern is almost vertical and completely intact, its handrail encrusted with stony coral. The rudder is an impressive sight and the huge four-bladed starboard screw propeller is even more spectacular.

Rarely on the *Umbria*, however, is the water very clear since the sea floor around the wreck is muddy and the current often reduces visibility - never with diasastrous effects, but sufficiently to be a hindrance when shooting panoramic views from a fair distance. The other screw has

C

C - Between the seats of one of the Fiat 1100 Lunga cars - their upholstery and padding long gone - encrusted with sediment, one can still notice the presence of the hand brake lever. Photograph by Andrea Ghisotti

D - Rows of large-calibre artillery ammunition can be seen through the semi-darkness; for obvious safety reasons, nothing must be touched while exploring the inner parts of the vessel.
Photograph by Andrea Ghisotti

E - The hundreds of bags of cement lined up in one of the holds now form a single, solid mass.
Photograph by Andrea Ghisotti

F - Caught in the beam of divers' torches are just a few of the 360,000 bombs stowed in the holds; they were the main component of the ship's cargo.
Photograph by Andrea Ghisotti

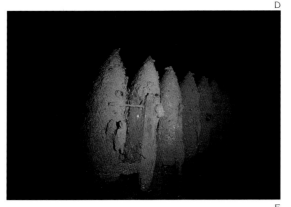

E

"Cordé per aereo" written on them. They must now be a rare item. You at last come to the forecastle, with its powerful winches, and finally to the narrow bow. A further excursion - though admittedly rather a long one - can be made towards the portside anchor, following the chain which, from the hawse hole, stretches 175 metres to the point where the anchor was dropped on that fateful morning of June 9, 1940.

F

G

still exist, especially in the case of the detonators. You should therefore float midwater and here, as in the other holds, be sure not to bring even the smallest "curios" away with you.

You can continue your exploration moving gradually towards the midships section where it is worth making a quick descent to the sea floor. Here, at a depth of about 35 metres, lie two splendid lifeboats - incredibly intact, with their lifejacket boxes still in place - as yet practically untouched by marine organisms. At their side is a huge air duct and all sorts of bits and pieces fallen from the wreck. But do not spend too long here or your visit to the forward holds will be necessarily cut short.

There are plenty of surprises in the central part of the ship. There are several large rooms, probably saloons, and two long corridors running parallel to the sides of the ship, with the passenger cabins off them. It's rather dark here and a good torch plus some experience of exploring wrecks are needed. You can also go down to the engine room, where there is a workshop

with a lathe as well - of course - as the huge engines. But this visit is only for people who do not suffer from claustrophobia and are not likely to be frightened by the dark and the murky water.

In front of the bridge are three more holds. In the first, closest to midships, numerous sacks of cement are piled up - and now form one single mass - and on the bottom of the hold, there are a great many bottles of wine; once there were also some nice little green bottles containing bergamot oil, but they have now disappeared. This is where the cars are, housed in an orlop deck, the first part of which is cluttered with a variety of items. It can be visited by no more than 2-3 divers at a time, as there is little space and discharged air bubbles make sediment come raining down.

The other holds contain all sorts of things: bottles, hanks of electrical wire, press-studs, aerial bombs, detonators and wooden boxes that are still sealed. Towards the bow there are some superb aircraft tyres, large in diameter but very narrow, with

G - In one of the holds are some wooden crates containing numerous glass jars, still packed in straw.
Photograph by Andrea Ghisotti

URANIA
by Andrea Ghisotti

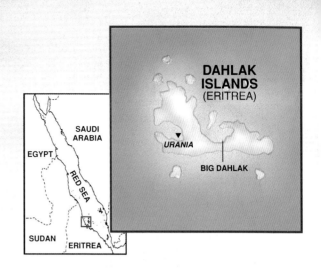

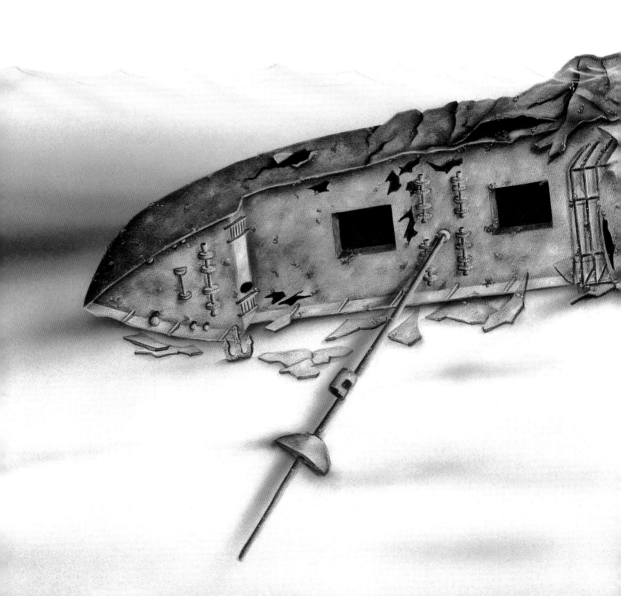

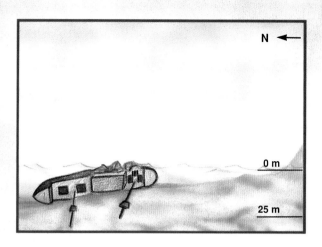

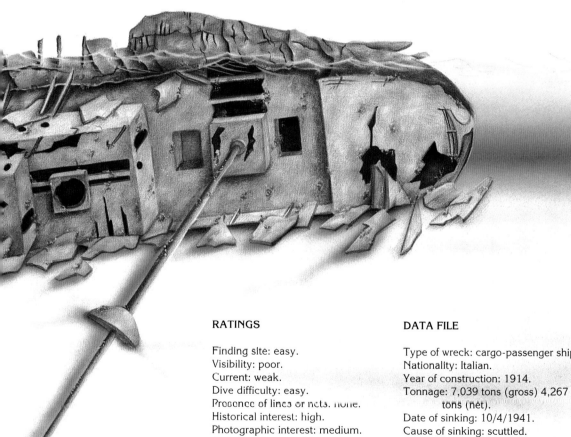

RATINGS

Finding site: easy.
Visibility: poor.
Current: weak.
Dive difficulty: easy.
Presence of lines or nets: none.
Historical interest: high.
Photographic interest: medium.
Biological interest: high.

DATA FILE

Type of wreck: cargo-passenger ship.
Nationality: Italian.
Year of construction: 1914.
Tonnage: 7,039 tons (gross) 4,267
    tons (net).
Date of sinking: 10/4/1941.
Cause of sinking: scuttled.
Site position: internal sea of Dahlak
    Kebir.
Geographical coordinates:
    10°39'52"N, 40°00'19"E.
Distance from shore: about half
    a mile.
Minimum depth: emerging from
    the surface.
Maximum depth: 25 metres.

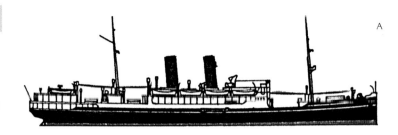
A

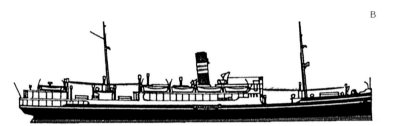
B

C

THE STEAMSHIP *URANIA*

Before relating the story of the *Urania*, our sincere thanks must go to several people without whose precious help and knowledge it would not have been possible to reconstruct the history of this vessel: Mr Duda who works in the archives of the Lloyd Triestino shipping company, and Mr Valenti, Mr Gellner and other members of the Associazione Marinara Aldebaran in Trieste.

The *Urania*, a mixed passenger-cargo steamship, was laid down on the building-slips at San Rocco di Muggia near Trieste on July 3, 1913 and launched on March 11,

1914 with the name *Hungaria*; it was officially handed over to its Austrian owners, the Lloyd Austriaco shipping line, on September 30, 1916 but remained in dock until the end of the war. The vessel was 125 metres long, 16 wide and 7.9 high, with gross and net tonnage of 7,039 and 4,267 tons respectively. It originally had two funnels but one had been added for aesthetic reasons only and was removed in 1922. The ship was fitted out to accommodate 133 first-class and 46 second-class passengers, with dining rooms, smoking rooms, music rooms and walkways below

and on deck for both classes. The ship's propulsion system was comprised of five boilers fired with liquid fuel and two triple-expansion engines producing 4,600 horsepower and giving the ship a top speed of 14.82 knots and a cruising speed of 12 knots (admittedly not exceptionally fast). After its sale to the Genoa-based Marittima Italiana line in 1923 it was renamed *Genova* and sailed under the Italian flag on routes to the East, with Bombay as its most frequent destination. It returned under the wing of Lloyd Triestino in 1932 when this company took

A, B, D, E, F - This series of drawings shows how the appearance of the ship changed over the years: launched in 1914 with the name of Hungaria, *it became the* Genova *in 1923 and eventually, in 1933, the* Urania. Photographs by Andrea Ghisotti, printed with kind permission of the Associazione Marinara Aldebaran

A - The Hungaria *in 1922, with two funnels.*

B - The Genova, *in 1923.*

C - This archive photo shows the steamship Urania *as she appeared from 1933 onwards, with black hull and white stem gunwhale.* Photograph by Andrea Ghisotti, printed with kind permission of the Lloyd's Triestino Historical Archive

over Marittima Italiana. Renamed *Urania*, it was modernized in 1934 with changes to its accommodation structures (it could now carry 60 passengers in first class, 139 in second, and 200 in third) and its gross tonnage was reduced to 4,870 tons. During the years of the war in Africa, the ship transported troops to Italy's colonies in East Africa, after which it was again used on the Red Sea and Indian Ocean routes. The *Urania* - like the *Umbria* and the *Nazario Sauro* - was trapped in the Red Sea when Italy entered World War II on June 10, 1940. When Eritrea was about to fall to the British, it took refuge amid the islands of the Great Dahlak Island, where it was scuttled on April 10, 1941.

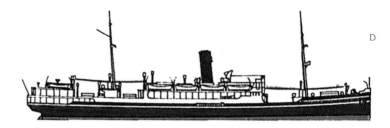

D

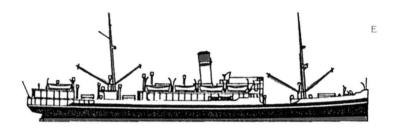

E

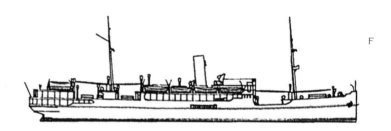

F

D - The Genova
in 1932, with all-black funnel.

E - The Urania
in 1933, with the gunwhale of the stem painted white.

F - The Urania
in 1938, with all-white hull.

Rediscovery and diving to the wreck

Once permission to visit the wrecks of the Italian ships scuttled at Ghubbet, in the Great Dahlak Island, had at last been obtained, actually finding the rusted remains of the *Urania* was no problem, since they emerge from the water and can be seen even from a distance. The vessel is lying on its port side at an angle of exactly 90°, so its starboard screw was initially above the surface (it disappeared from the site, together with the port screw, soon after the end of the war). Much has changed since the '50s, when photos of the scene were taken by Lino Pellegrini, a journalist. The structures have collapsed in several places and the fine-looking stern with its railings and handrail, clearly visible in those pictures, has now mostly vanished beneath the surface. The biggest surprise, however, was to find the bridge on the right side of the wreck, with the

G - Locating the Urania is not difficult since the wreck emerges from the surface; it is lying on its port side in the shallow waters off the Great Dahlak Island.

G

A

We found two pairs of white-bellied storks nesting there, herons, kingfishers, gannets, terns and seagulls, as well as countless birds making brief stops before flying on. Wearing just mask and fins it is easier to make your way amid the sharp girders where the vessel is only partly submerged and you can explore the engine room with its huge piston rods and the crankshaft which continues towards the stern with the propeller shafts. When descending with full gear it is best to explore in a clockwise direction, making for the stern, where the propeller shaft supports and the remains of the huge rudder are an impressive sight. Occasionally visibility can be as good as 20 metres but as

A - The parts of the Italian steamship still above water have now turned a deep ochre-brown, in splendid contrast to the intense blue of the surrounding sea; the vessel was scuttled in April 1941 so as not to let it fall into British hands.

B - More than fifty years have passed since the vessel sank and thick concretions now cover its twisted plates.

B

C - In the past few years the ship's structures have collapsed in several places and the stern - previously almost entirely above water - has now sunk below the surface; the photo reveals, in the background, the mast of a ferry-boat which sank close to the Urania.

C

D

D - A school of glassfish swim among the remains of the ship; the Urania has a dense and varied population of marine creatures.

mast emerging from the water. We racked our brains for an explanation but it wasn't until we had donned mask and fins and dived in to take a closer look that we found one: for reasons we shall never know, another vessel - a large reinforced-concrete ferry-boat used to carry fuel and materials - had sunk right beside the old steamship. It is worth taking a good look at the part above the surface before starting to explore underwater.
Numerous colonies of birds have settled on the wreck amid the old metal structures, which have now turned a most attractive colour.

E

E - In the forward section of the ship are countless holes made by explosions, shrapnel and bullets; in 1941 the crews of several British aircraft apparently mistook the still emerging wrecked ship for a sea-worthy enemy vessel and launched an attack on it.

F, G - After long withstanding the force of the waves and erosion, the stern eventually collapsed and sank to the bottom, a tangle of distorted girders, plates and railings.

H - Just discernible in this photo is the crosstree of the mizzenmast, which lies at full length on the seabed; abundant plankton explains the disturbingly green colour of the water.

I - The fairly well preserved foremast is also practically resting on the bottom in this site's shallow waters; its crow's nest can be seen in this picture.

G

F

H

I

a rule, the water around the wreck is murky and plentiful plankton makes it permanently green. Lying on the seabed a short way forward from the poop deck is one of the two masts and, nearby, a small swimming pool; this was built in a former cargo hatch during the 1934 refit when, as Valenti told us, amenities for passengers were upgraded. A bathtub can also be made out close by. This brings you to the quarterdeck, now offering little besides a mass of tangled structures on the seabed. This is the last part of the ship emerging from the water which now gets progressively deeper, from 10-13 metres at the stern to about 20 metres at this point. The foremast is still intact with its crow's nest and crosstrees. At its base you can make out the winches once used to move the cargo handling booms. Before reaching the bow you will notice - on the bottom - an enormous, chainless, Hall-type 3.5 ton anchor, presumably the spare bow anchor. Still intact and adorned with sea-whips, the bow is an

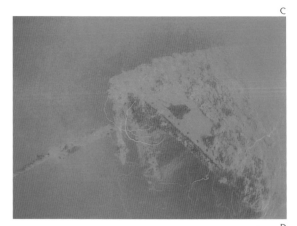

impressive sight. There is much less of interest on opposite side of the vessel, with the keel and starboard flank. Its fascination lies instead in the incredibly thick hard coral encrustations which coat the entire metal structure; they provide a home for numerous lifeforms, seemingly transforming the hull into a coral reef. There is a very large hole - about 2x2 m - in the starboard flank, probably made by the explosive charges used to scuttle the ship. In the forward section of the deck too there are numerous holes caused by explosions, which could have been left by practice shots fired by the Ethiopians or by a British air raid in 1941, reported in several

A - Standing upright in the midst of debris from the ship, just in front of the bow, is a huge, chainless Hall anchor, very probably a spare bow anchor that, due to its weight, broke away from its chain and plummeted to the bottom.

B - Much of the wreck is now no more than a maze of twisted girders: divers exploring the interior must watch out for sharp edges that could cause injury and must avoid stirring up the thick layers of sediment.

C - The submerged parts of the ship are completely covered in a thick coat of corals - hard and soft coral formations and splendid sea fans - making the wreck look like part of a reef.

D, E - The quarterdeck and holds were violently shaken by the explosion to scuttle the ship and by the subsequent collapse of its flanks; nevertheless, inside them one can still make out many structural elements and pieces of equipment.

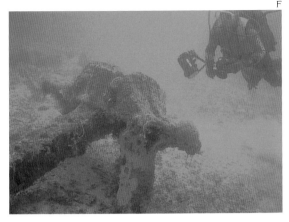

F

G

documents. Experienced divers can complete their visit by finning their way down the anchor chains. The water gets no deeper than 25 metres but make allowance for finning at least 350 metres in all (there and back) to see the starboard anchor, and a further 200 metres to get to the port anchor. The effort is well worthwhile since every single link of the chain is densely populated with sea creatures: anenomes, sea lilies, sea squirts, hard corals, sponges, diadem sea urchins, crustaceans and fish - a whole explosion of marine life crowned by the two superb anchors, embedded in the floor of the sea ever since they were dropped there in April 1941.

The two chains crisscross again and again before heading in different directions; with its arms completely covered by brightly coloured sea lilies, the anchor at the end of the right-hand chain is truly spectacular.

H

I

F - A diver examines one of the two huge anchors, dropped shortly before the Urania *was scuttled in April 1941, and now encrusted with corals and sea lilies.*

G - In the engine room the biggest thrill is seeing the engines themselves, with the huge piston rods and crankshaft still in full view.

H, I - Incredible clumps of brightly coloured sponges and sea lilies have colonized numerous parts of the wreck, making it look like an enchanted, flower-filled garden.

J - In one of the ship's bathrooms, practically entirely encrusted with marine organisms, tiling produced with small tesserae could almost be taken for some strange modern work of art.

All the photos of the dive to the Urania *were taken by Andrea Ghisotti.*

J

NAZARIO SAURO
by Andrea Ghisotti

RATINGS

Finding site: easy.
Visibility: poor.
Current: variable.
Dive difficulty: medium.
Presence of lines or nets: none.
Historical interest: high.
Photographic interest: high.
Biological interest: high.

DATA FILE

Type of wreck: cargo-passenger ship.
Nationality: Italian.
Year of construction: 1921.
Tonnage: 8,150 tons (gross) 4,491
       tons (net).
Date of sinking: 6/4/1941 or
       10/4/1941.
Cause of sinking: scuttled.
Site position: close to Dahlak
       Kebir island.
Distance from shore: about one mile.
Minimum depth: 3 metres.
Maximum depth: 39 metres.

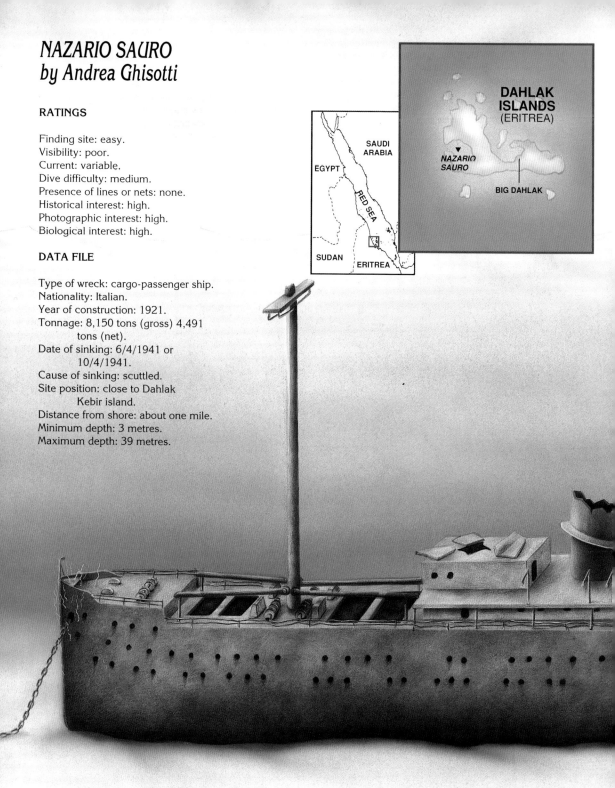

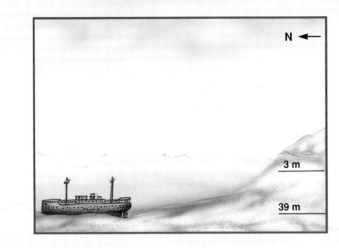

THE STEAMSHIP
NAZARIO SAURO

How does one go about reconstructing the history of a ship 75 years old? In our case it would have been an impossible task but for the help of Mr Duda who, at an age when most people have joined the ranks of pensioners, is still at work in the archives of the Lloyd

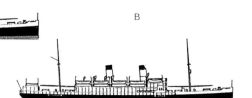

A

A - In this archive photo the Nazario Sauro *is seen with the colours of the Transatlantica Italiana line, with conspicuous white stars painted on the funnels.*

B

Triestino shipping line, for the sheer love of it. Invaluable contributions were also made by members of the Associazione Marinara Aldebaran in Trieste - especially its chairman Mr Valenti, and Mr Gellner - who have an amazing knowledge of ships and navigation. Thanks to help received from these dedicated people we are able to tell the story of this awe-inspiring wreck. Building work on the steamship *Nazario Sauro* - sister-ship of the *Cesare Battisti*, the *Ammiraglio Bettolo* and the *Leonardo da Vinci* - started in 1919 in the Ansaldo yards at Sestri Ponente, in Italy; it was initially intended to be a cargo ship but while still under construction, its interior was re-designed as a passenger ship for emigrants. There was accommodation for 80 first-class passengers, in comfortable single and twin-bedded cabins, with many amenities (bars, rooms for dining, smoking, writing and music, areas on deck for exercise and recreation) and 48 second-class passengers, in twin- and four-bedded cabins, with their own saloon and dining room. The ship was fitted out to carry no fewer than 1,109 emigrants in third class, in accommodation comprised mainly of dormitories-cum-living quarters with little in the way of "mod cons". The ship was 136 metres long, 16 wide and 9.47 high, with a 5.22 m draught when

C

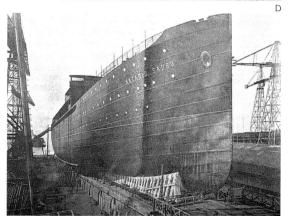

D

B - These drawings show how the Nazario Sauro *looked at three different moments during its life. Above, the* Nazario Sauro *in 1924, when it was owned by the Società Transatlantica Italiana. At the centre, the steamship in 1935, with the colours of the Tirrenia line. Below, the ship in 1938, the year after its sale to Lloyd Triestino. Photograph by Andrea Ghisotti, printed with kind permission of the Associazione Marinara Aldebaran*

C, D - When these photos were taken in 1920, the Nazario Sauro *was still in the Ansaldo shipbuilding yard; the great steamship was launched in 1921. Photographs by Andrea Ghisotti, printed with kind permission of the Associazione Marinara Aldebaran*

empty and 8.22 with a full load. It had a gross tonnage of 8,150 tons, a net tonnage of 4,491 tons and a carrying capacity of 4,669 tons. Apparently its engine system was originally based on 6 coal-fired boilers but these were later replaced with 4 oil-fired boilers, and two groups of three turbines producing 7,900 horsepower and giving the ship a top speed of 15 knots and a cruising speed of about 13 knots. The *Nazario Sauro* was commissioned from the Ansaldo shipyards in Sestri Ponente by Trasatlantica Italiana (the vessel was named - by the way - after an Italian World War I hero, captured and hanged by the Austrians who, because of his Istrian origin, considered him a deserter). Launched on May 14, 1921, the ship was actually handed over to its owners only on February 1, 1924, by which time Trasatlantica Italiana had serious financial problems. That same month of February the *Nazario Sauro* made its maiden voyage from Genoa to Mar del Plata under

F

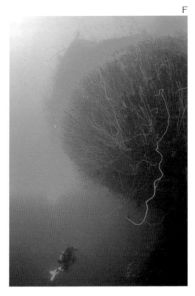

G - Its rails still just visible beneath the mantle of sea whips, the quarterdeck has a ghostlike appearance in the murky water.

H - This photograph reveals the base of the foremast, with the derricks now lying horizontal.

I - A diver illuminates part of the bridge deck, revealing the elegant design of this area of the Italian steamship. The waters in and about the wreck are alive with fish, perhaps because few fishermen and scuba divers are ever seen around these parts; frequently spotted here are huge jacks, silvery barracuda, giant manta and big snappers.

G

E

E - Still practically upright, the vessel lies on the sandy bottom at a depth of 40 metres; highlighted in this photograph is the bridge deck, with the windows of the officers' quarters.

F - The gigantic stern of the ship is smothered by a tangle of sea whips; viewed from below, it looks even more imposing. A very effective impression of the ship's huge size is conveyed by the small figure of the diver.

H

I

A - The bow of the wreck has a sharp cutwater and a rather tapered look, typical of ships built in the first part of the century.

B - The forward funnel must once have been really large; its metal cladding has now been almost entirely eaten away by the corrosive effect of the sea water and only a skeleton structure remains.

C - Although thick with concretions, the forward anchor-hoist is still intact. Near this part of the wreck the anchor chains can still be seen, stretching away into the gloomy depths and soon out of sight.

D - A diver stares in wonder at the huge bow of the Nazario Sauro. In view of the colossal size of this steamship (136 metres long, 16 wide and 9.47 high), anyone keen to explore every possible corner of the wreck and discover all its secrets is advised to plan several dives.

B

the command of Captain Canepa. By now, however, these ships were unable to compete with the much faster and more comfortable new transatlantic liners operated by Navigazione Generale Italiana and Lloyd Sabaudo. At the end of 1927 the *Nazario Sauro* was consequently taken out of commission. It remained in mothballs until 1934 when Tirrenia became its owner and refitted it internally, with accommodation for only 576 third-class passengers. In 1935 it started to sail regularly to the Italian colony of Somalia, stopping en route at Massawa in Eritrea to unload troops and material during the Ethiopian campaign.

On January 1, 1937 it acquired a new owner and a new look: Lloyd Triestino - which had obtained all the shipping concessions for Italian Eastern Africa - painted it white (from its previous black), traditional colour of all the vessels operated by the Trieste-based shipping line. At the outbreak of war on June 10, 1940 the *Nazario Sauro*, like many other cargo and passenger ships, was caught in the Red Sea. It remained in mothballs in Massawa until April of the following year, when Eritrea was about to fall to the British. It then moved to the Great Dahlak Island, where it was scuttled on April 6, 1941 (April 10 according to other sources).

Rediscovery of the wreck

Few of the adventures I have experienced as a "wreck hunter" can equal the thrill of finding and exploring the *Nazario Sauro*. We knew of the existence of the wreck although our information conflicted with the records of the Italian Navy, which reported it "recovered by the British". In the '50s the foremast still emerged above the surface and the first divers to come this way descended to visit the vessel. Among them was Jacques Cousteau: he described it as extremely interesting, and it was so thoroughly covered with white sea-whips that he called it the "hoary-haired wreck". But Cousteau did not know its name and the murky water made it impossible for him to film it. Later, for twenty years or so, the Ghubbet Sea in the midst of the Great Dahlak Island was made strictly off-limits, partly on account of the war being fought in the area but mainly because a Soviet military base had been installed there. When the war at last ended, a few years ago, we repeatedly tried to get permission to visit the wrecks of ships scuttled in these waters, but without success. Then one day, almost miraculously, the long-awaited permits arrived. In a flash I was busy organizing an expedition with Riccardo Melotti, companion of many of my

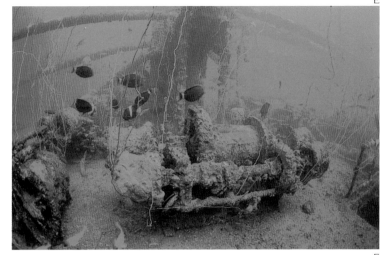

E - Still clearly visible at the base of the foremast are the winches used to manoeuvre the cargo booms.

F, G - Prominent in these photos are the large air ducts at the four corners of the skylight at the centre of the bridge deck.

A - In the semi-darkness the deck appears to be overrun by sea whips and antipatharia, of a size that never ceases to amaze

B - Exuberantly growing sea whips of the Gorgonacea *order have totally changed the appearance of this forward bitt; thanks to the profusion of these coelenterates with their hornlike skeletons, Jacques-Yves Cousteau nicknamed the* Nazario Sauro *the "hoary-haired wreck".*

C - Left lying on deck in the bow section of the ship, this huge cable is now so thickly encrusted as to be almost unrecognizable. Nestling between the hard coral formations on the left of the picture is a fine specimen of sea anemone, with the inevitable clownfish hovering above it; around and about are other denizens of the Red Sea: angelfish and numerous surgeonfish.

A

B

C

D - A diver examines the binnacle of the compass; beside it is the speaking tube used to communicate with the engine room. The engine system of the Nazario Sauro was comprised of four oil-fired boilers and two sets of turbines, capable of producing a top speed of 15 knots.

E - On the quarterdeck are two cumbersome - and now extensively damaged - structures which could possibly once have been large water tanks.

F - There are more exciting discoveries in store when exploring the far end of the stern: for instance, the remains of the emergency rudder.

adventures: he has spent many years in Eritrea and we have used his beautiful house in Massawa as a base for all our expeditions in the region. By now however the mast of the Nazario Sauro had disappeared and our search for the wreck - including a day spent with a Danakil fisherman who swore he knew its exact site - proved fruitless. But after days of tedious searching with a sonic depth finder, our luck changed: the marker suddenly shot upwards, just as if there was a cathedral built on the desolately flat seabed. I shall never forget my first dive, equipped with just mask and fins, to tie a line from our dinghy to the crosstree of the mast, only 3 metres below the

surface: all around me in the cloudy black water were hundreds of fish - leaping jacks, barracudas, mantas, snappers and enormous sea breams.
The Nazario Sauro lay waiting for us just a few metres further down, in an atmosphere of tremendous gloom but - unbelievably - still in one piece. We were the first divers to explore it again after so many years and to set eyes on its incredible mantle of gorgonians, so thick in places that access to its interiors was quite impossible.

Diving to the wreck

The ship is too big to be thoroughly
explored in a single dive unless
you remain on deck, at a depth of
25 metres. But it is definitely worth
paying a visit to the bow and stern
which - still in perfect order - are
resting on the flat bottom, about
40 metres from the surface.
The bow has a sharp cutwater from
which the anchor chains stretch
seawards; hanging from the thick,
hoary "mane" of sea-whips
encrusting its surface are hundreds
of huge mollusks, their dead shells
scattered on the seabed all around.
We had a disappointment when
exploring the stern since the two
screws had disappeared, carried
off after the war by an Italian
recovery firm. But the rudder -
of the semi-balanced type - is still
in its place, though the bottom part
is now corroded.
The superstructures are simply
splendid, with all the lifeboat davits
in position, remains of the two
gigantic funnels, various decks,
enormous air ducts and extractors,
as well as the two masts with their

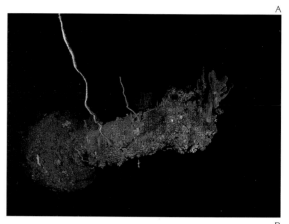

A

B

C

crow's nests and derricks.
The wooden bridge has regrettably
succumbed to corrosion but there
is a second superb binnacle, still
with its compass and speaking
tube; the auxiliary steering
apparatus is also still in its place.
A no less fascinating experience
is to explore the interior of the
Nazario Sauro, with its numerous
washbasins, tables, autoclaves,
portholes, stairways and countless
items of furniture and equipment,
which I sincerely hope any visitors
will leave strictly "as is" for the joy
of future generations of scuba
divers.

D

*All the photos
of the dive to the
Nazario Sauro
were taken by
Andrea Ghisotti.*

E - As well as the great colonies of sea whips, numerous exquisitely coloured sea anemones now populate the structures of the wreck.

F - China plates and dishes - often still in one piece - litter the galley floor, adding a special pathos to these places where one can seemingly still relive the life on board.

G - This two-bowl sink with well-preserved taps is in what was probably the ship's laundry. Originally built as a cargo ship and later refitted to carry passengers, the Nazario Sauro *provided accommodation for 80 passengers in first class, 48 in second and 1,109 in third. In 1934, after the Tirrenia shipping line bought the vessel, its capacity in third class was reduced to 576.*

140 A diver hovers over the bow of the Carnatic, *a fine-looking British steamer that sank on the Sha'ab Abu Nuhâs reef in 1876.*

COVER
The stern of the Ghiannis D., which sunk in 1968, rests at 89 feet deep.
Photograph by Kurt Amsler

BACK COVER TOP LEFT
Small schoolds of corbs frequent the wreck of the Jolanda.
Photograph by Roberto Rinaldi

BACK COVER TOP RIGHT
The Thistlegorm, bombed and sunk in 1941, is today one of the more famous wrecks in the Red Sea.
Photograph by Roberto Rinaldi

BACK COVER BOTTOM
The Ghiannis D. sits split in half on the sea floor at Abu Nuhas.
Drawing by Cristina Franco